MARCH 50 COLORING PAGES
FOR OLDER KIDS RELAXATION

SHIH CHIEN HUA

PUBLISHED BY:
SHIH CHIEN HUA
Copyright © 2018

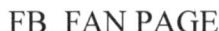

SEABIRD SHOP >50FOR

FB FAN PAGE

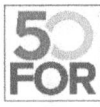

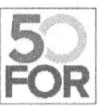

Disclaimer

The information contained in this book is for general information purposes only. The information is provided by the authors and while we endeavor to keep the information up to date and correct, we make no representations or warranties of any kind, express or implied, about the completeness, accuracy, reliability, suitability or availability with respect to the book or the information, products, services, or related graphics contained in the book for any purpose. Any reliance you place on such information is therefore strictly at your own risk.

MARCH 1ST

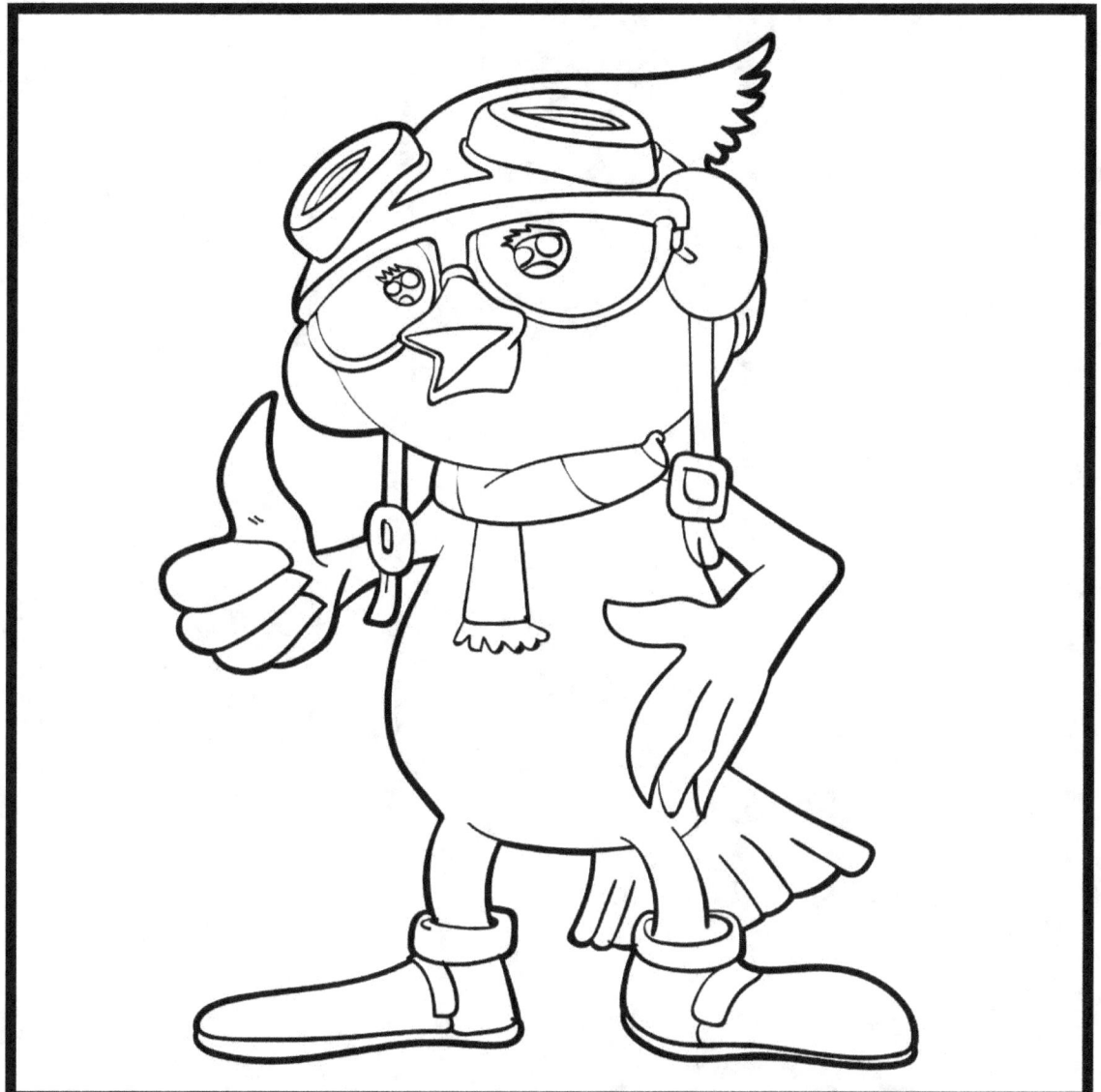

note:

_____

_____

_____

MARCH 2ND

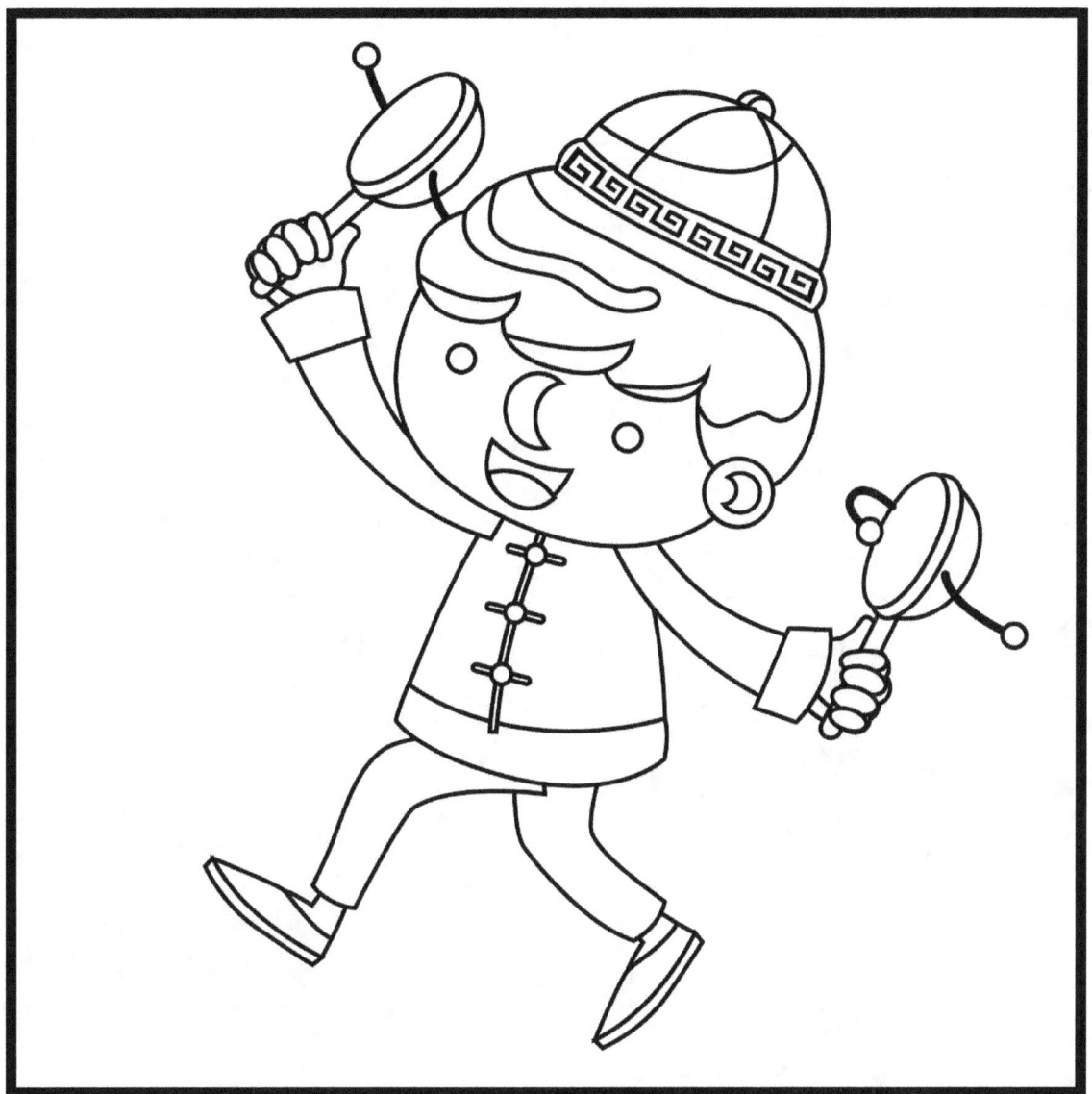

note:

_____

_____

_____

MARCH 3RD

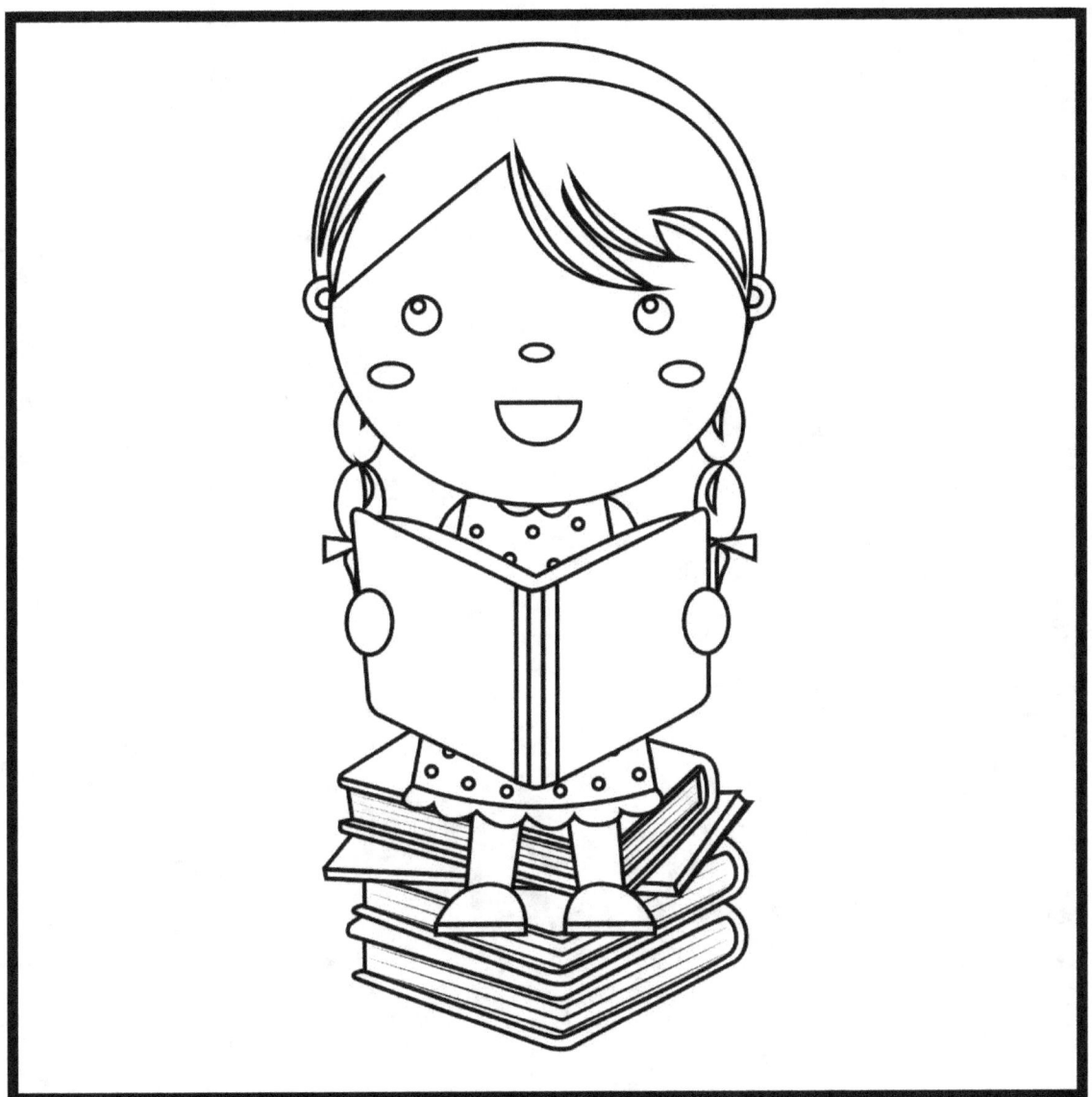

note:

_____

_____

_____

MARCH 4TH

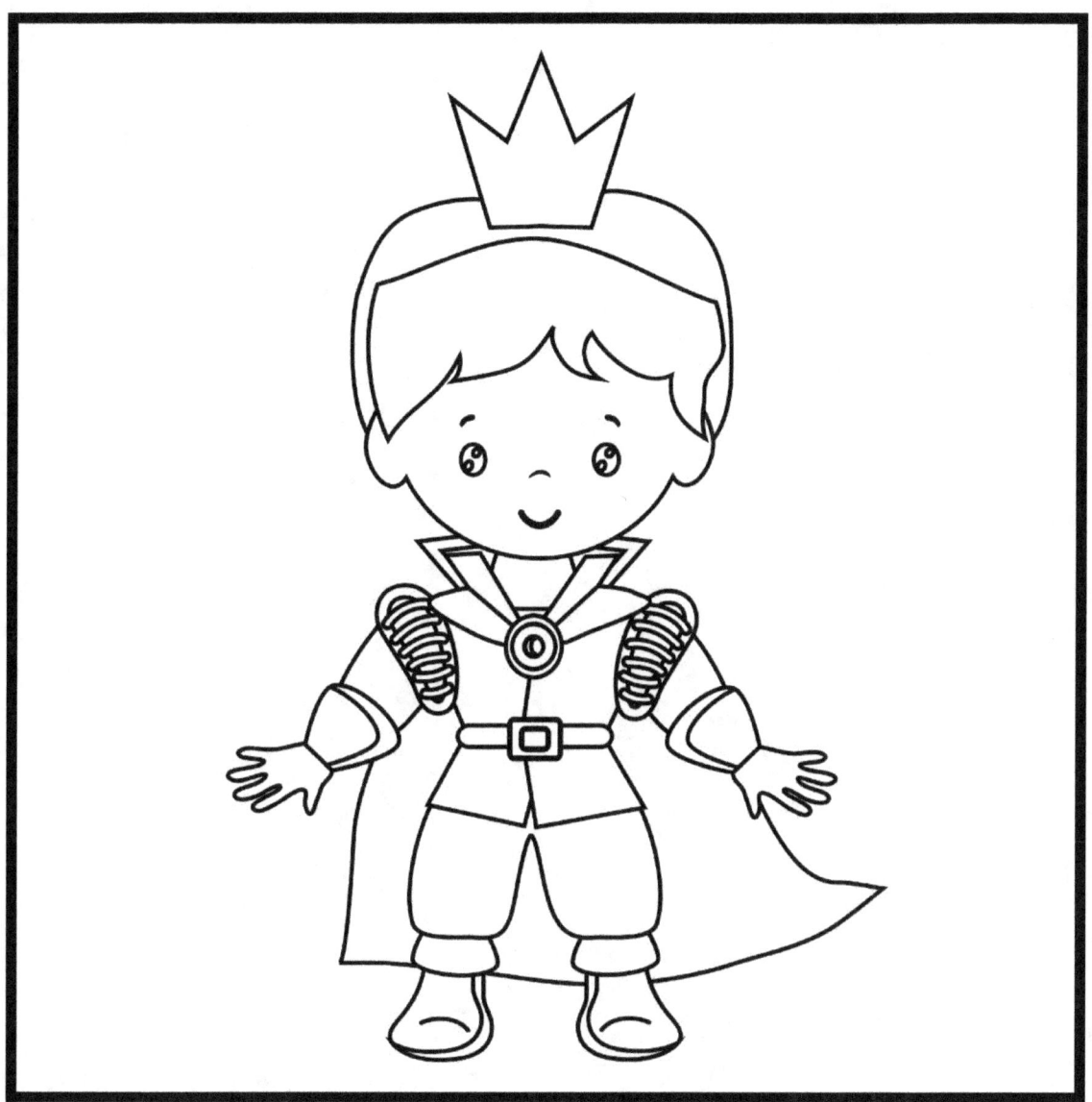

note:

_____

_____

_____

MARCH 5TH

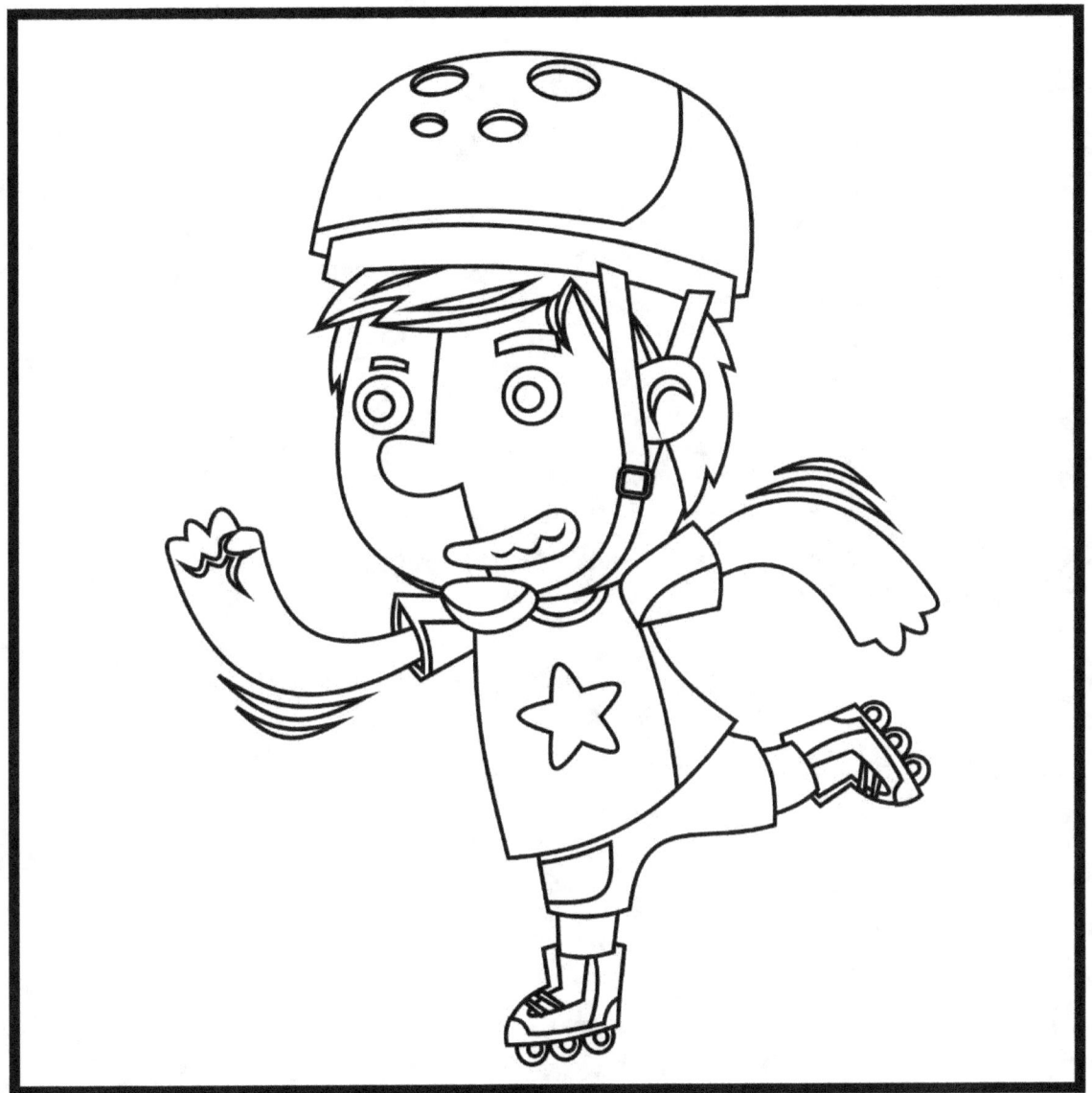

note:

_____

_____

_____

MARCH 6TH

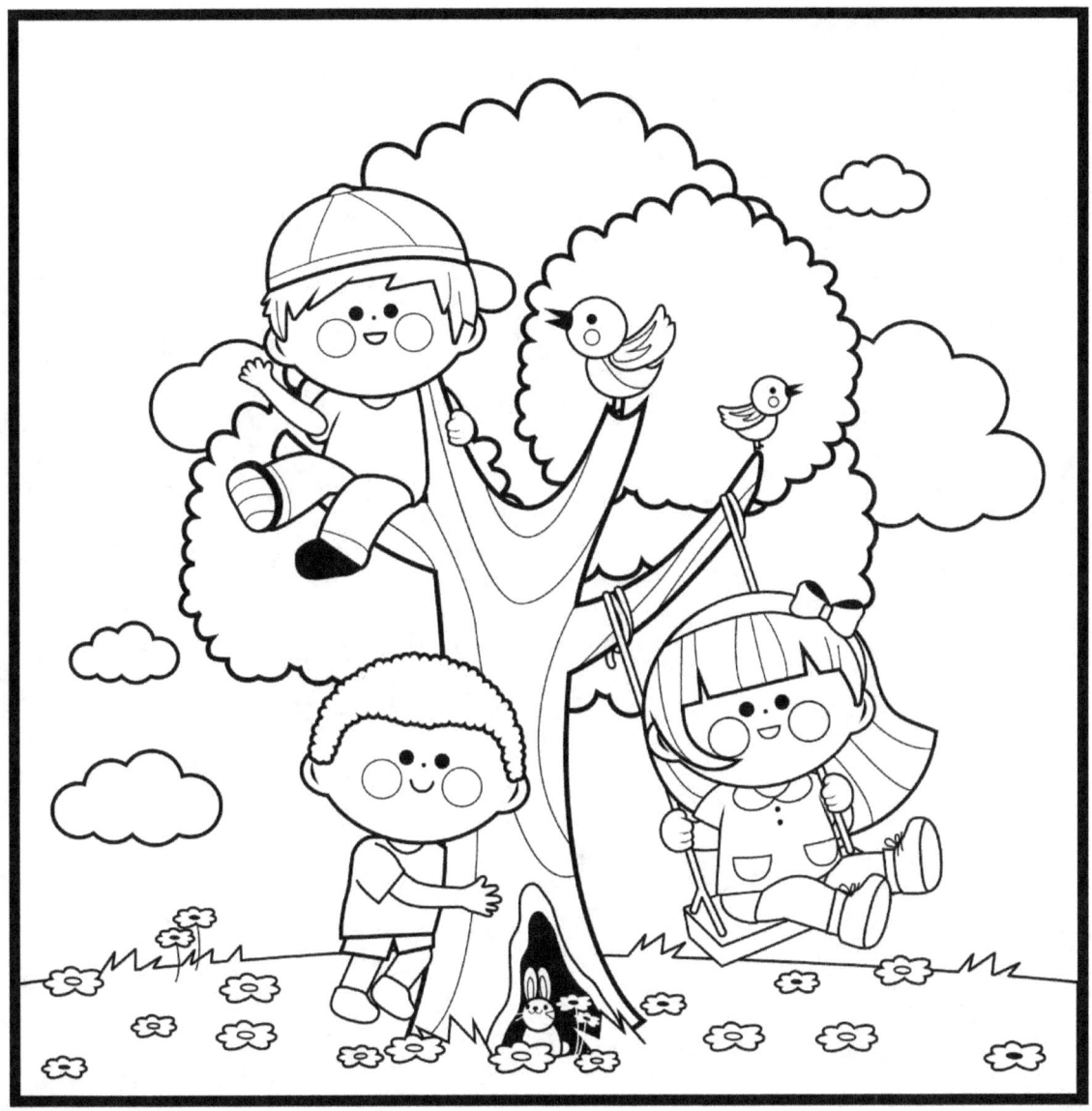

note:

_____

_____

_____

MARCH 7TH

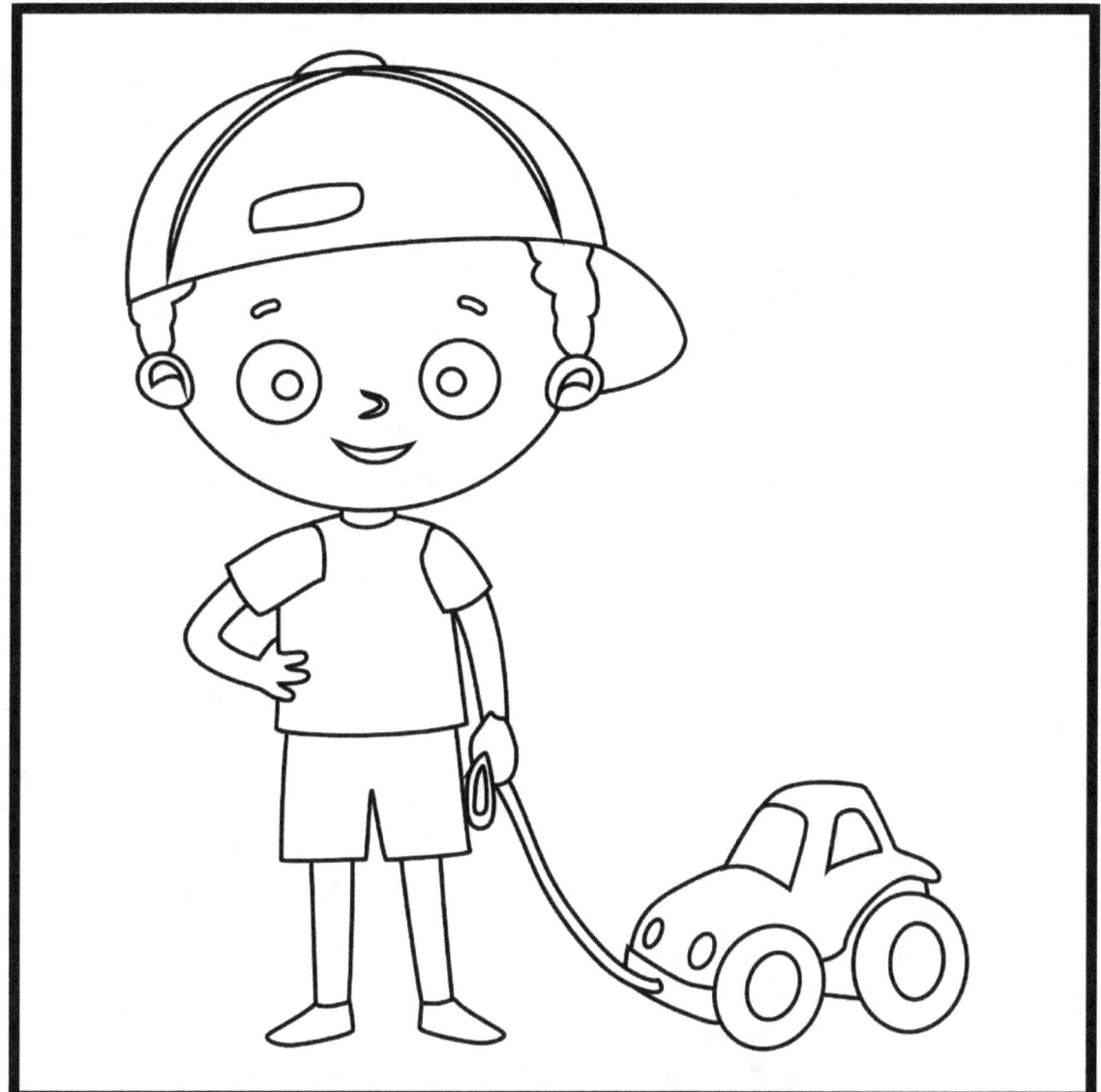

note:

_____

_____

_____

MARCH 8TH

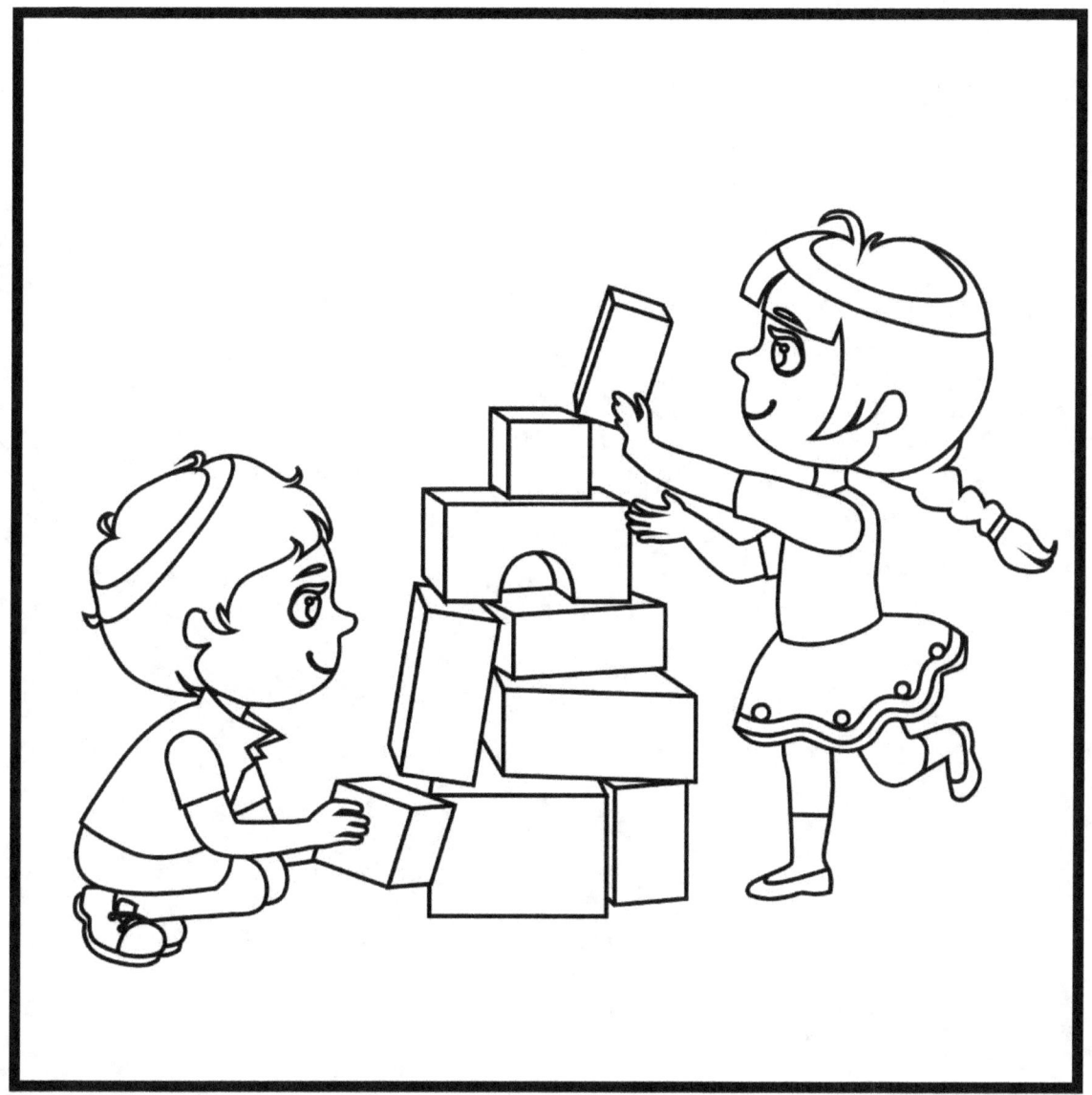

note:

_____

_____

_____

MARCH 9TH

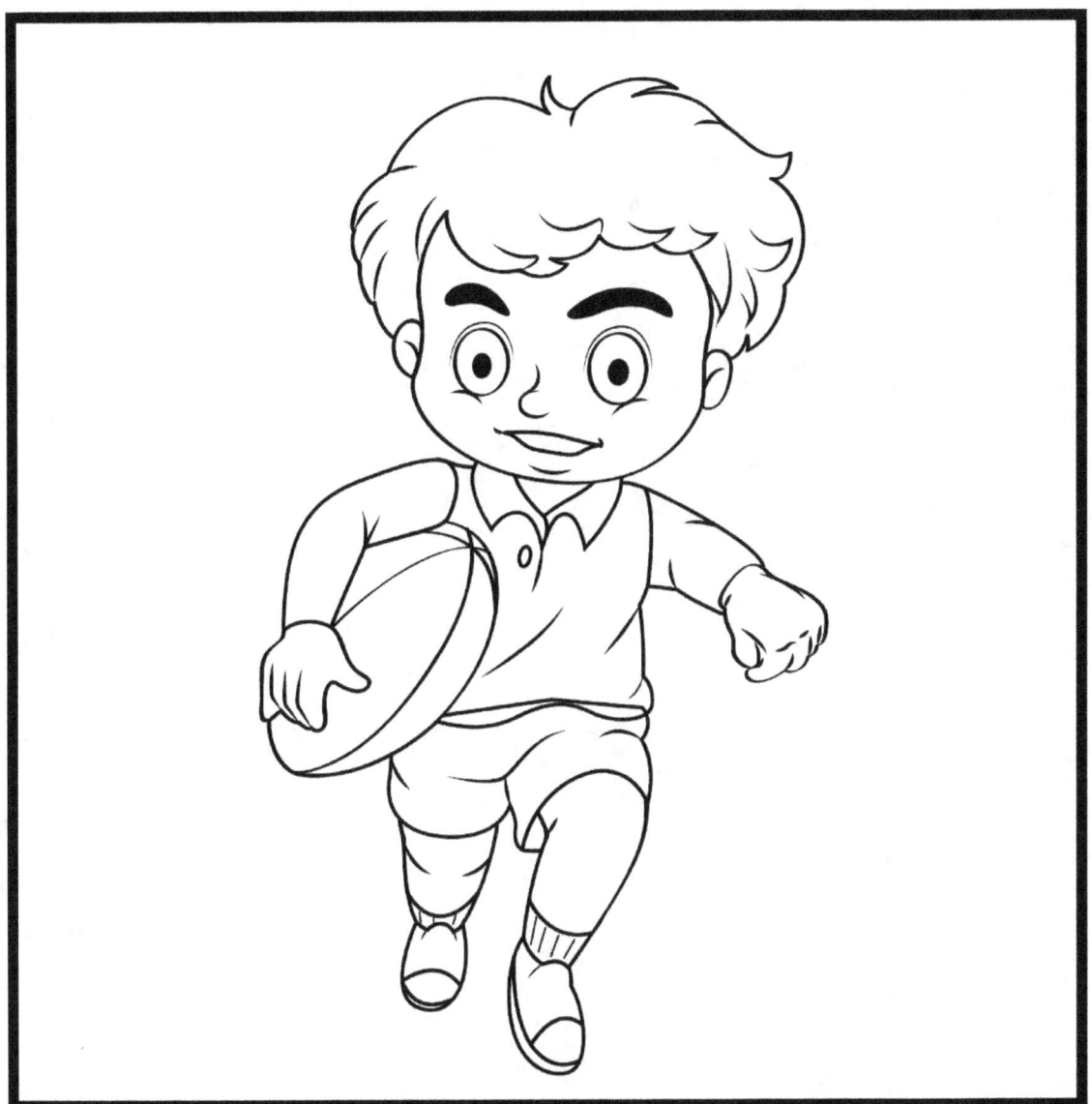

note:

_____

_____

_____

MARCH 10TH

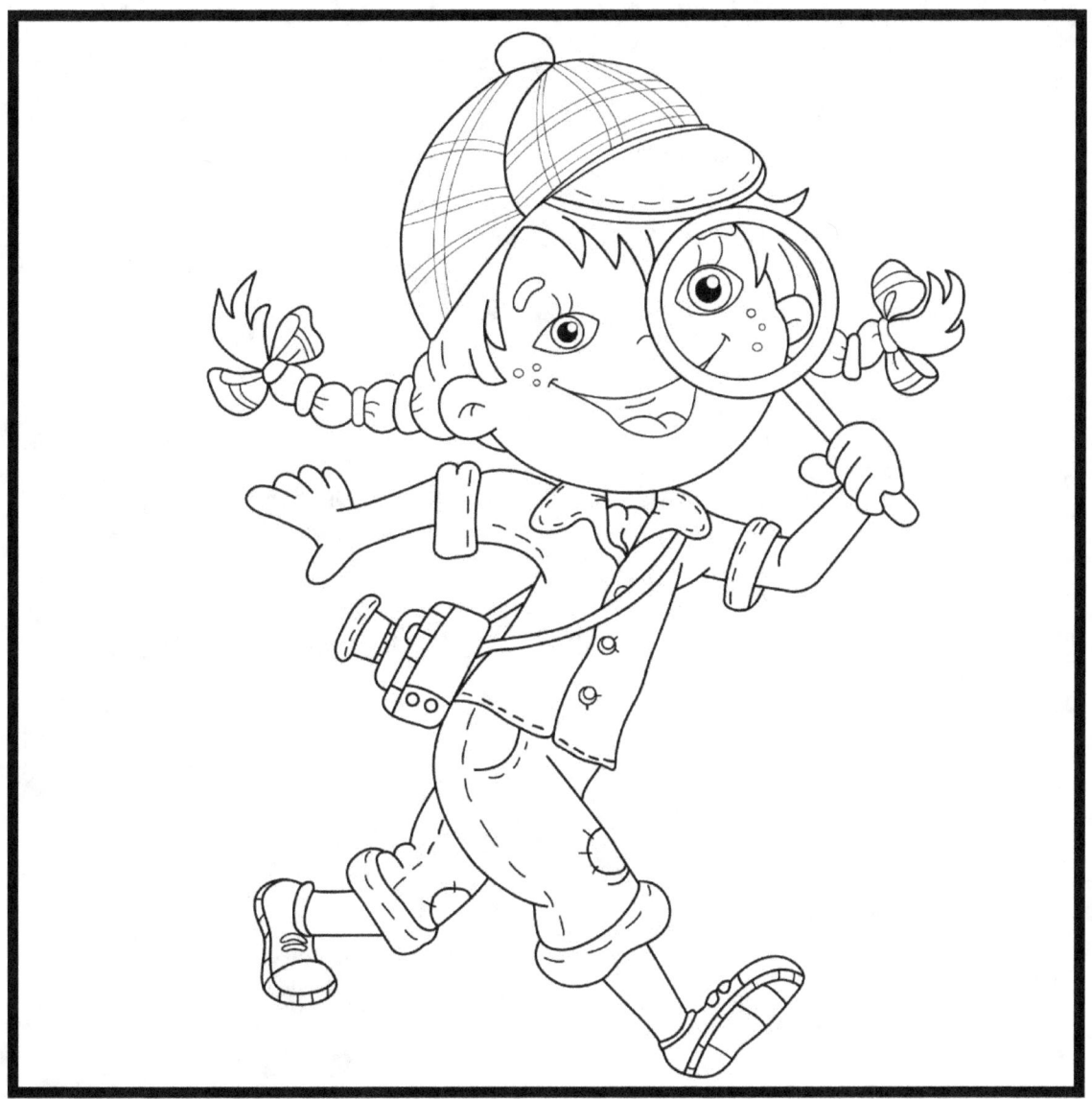

note:

_____

_____

_____

MARCH 11TH

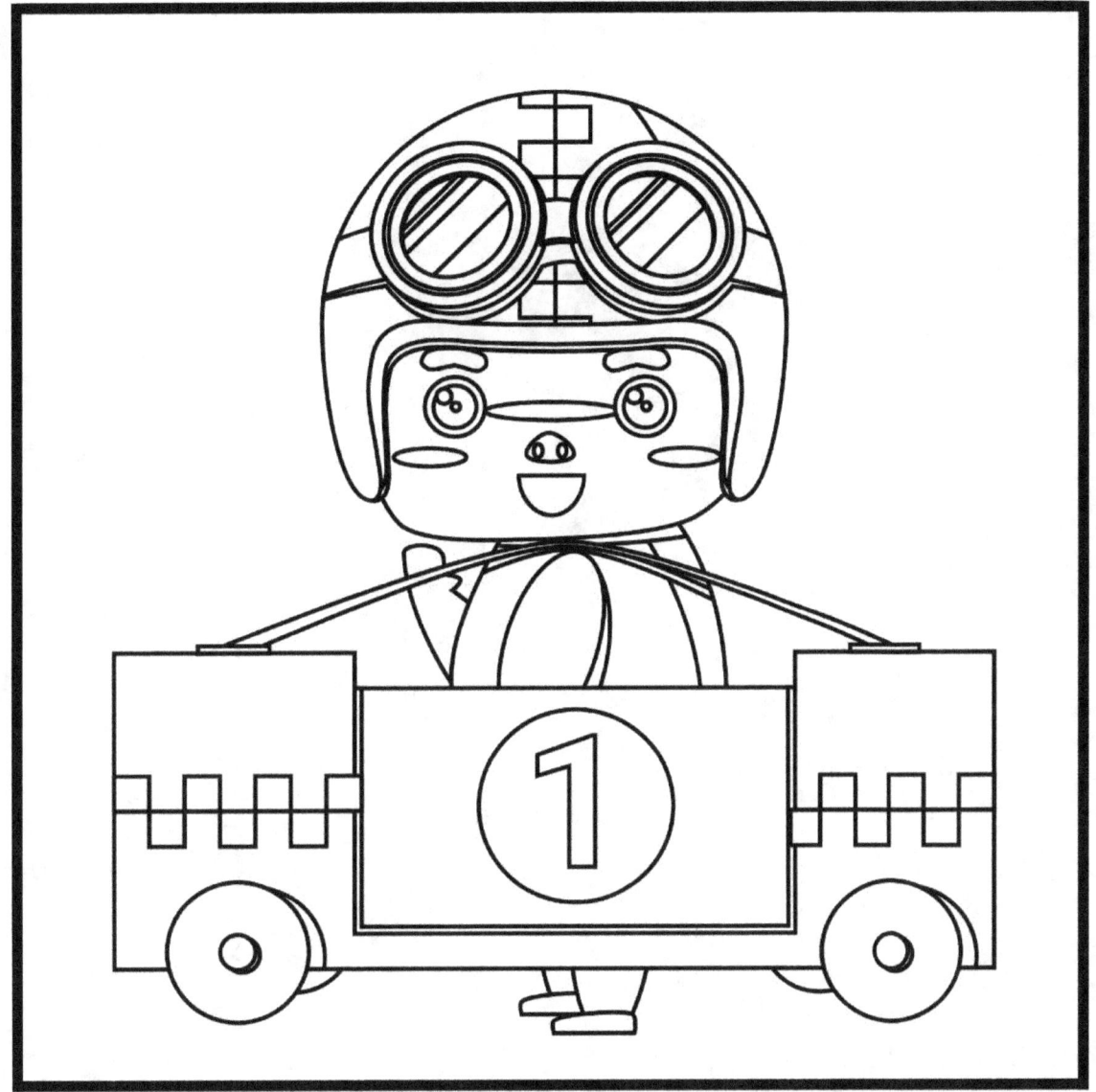

note:

_____

_____

_____

MARCH 12TH

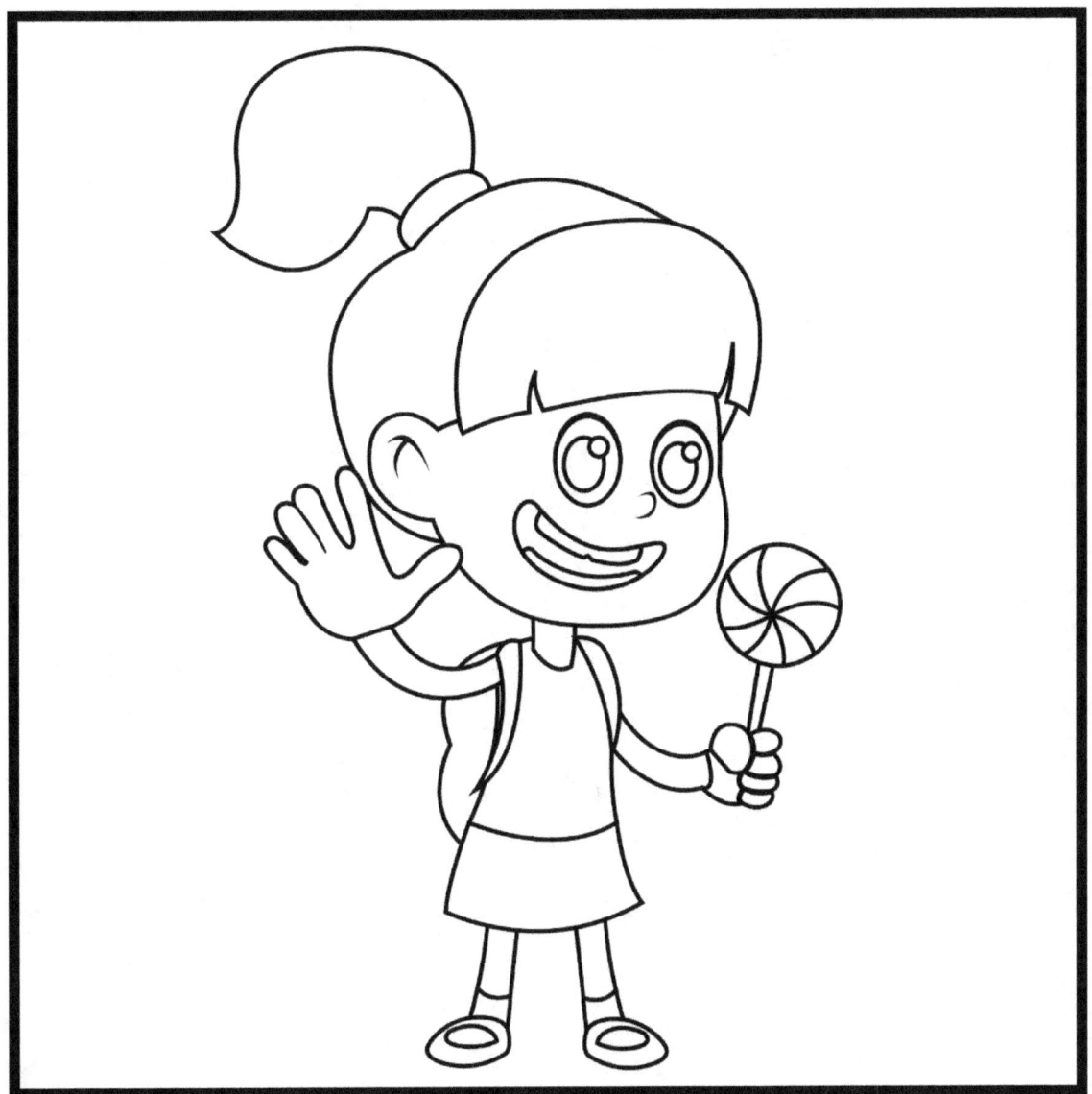

note:

_____

_____

_____

MARCH 13TH

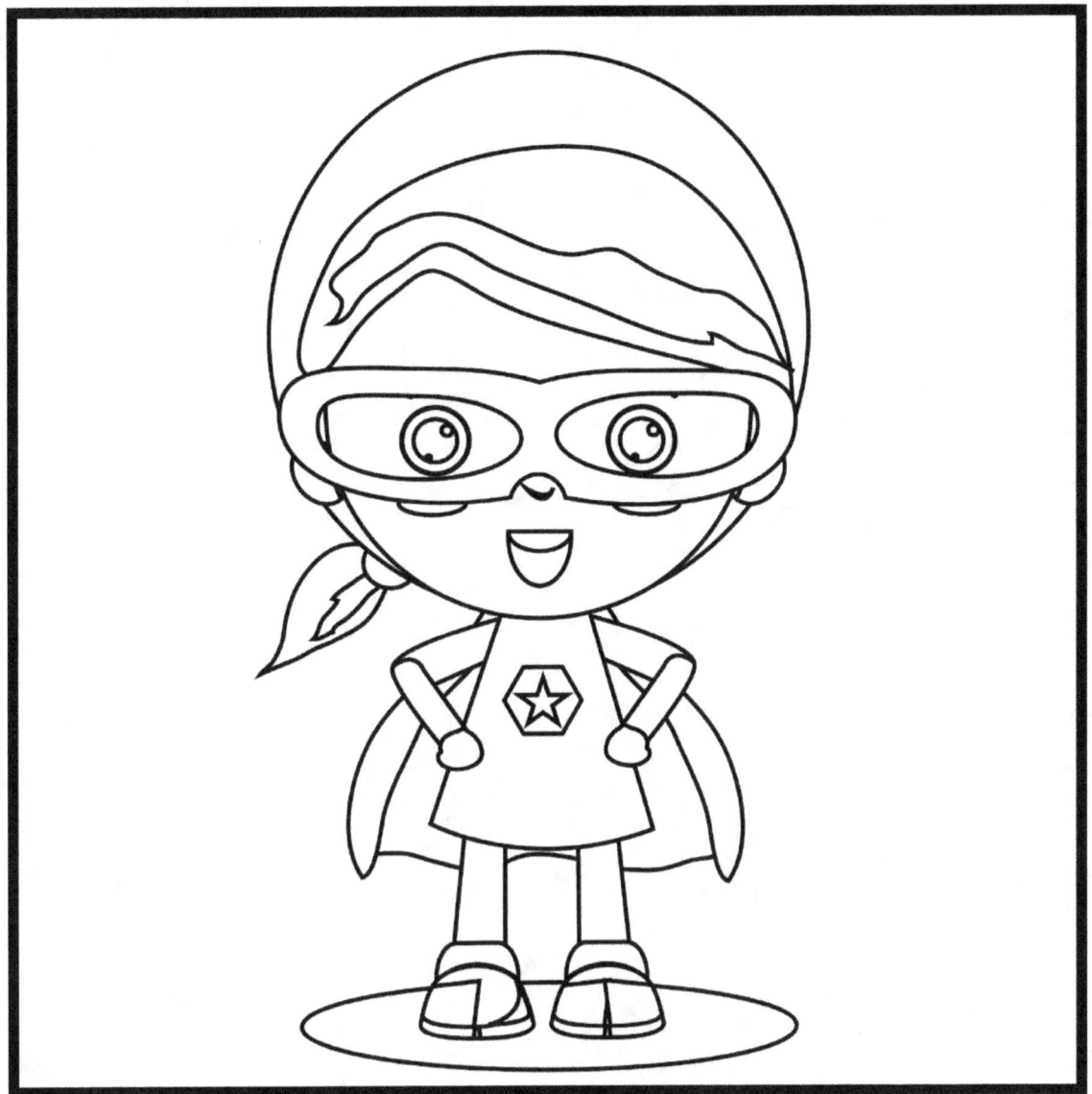

note:

_____

_____

_____

MARCH 14TH

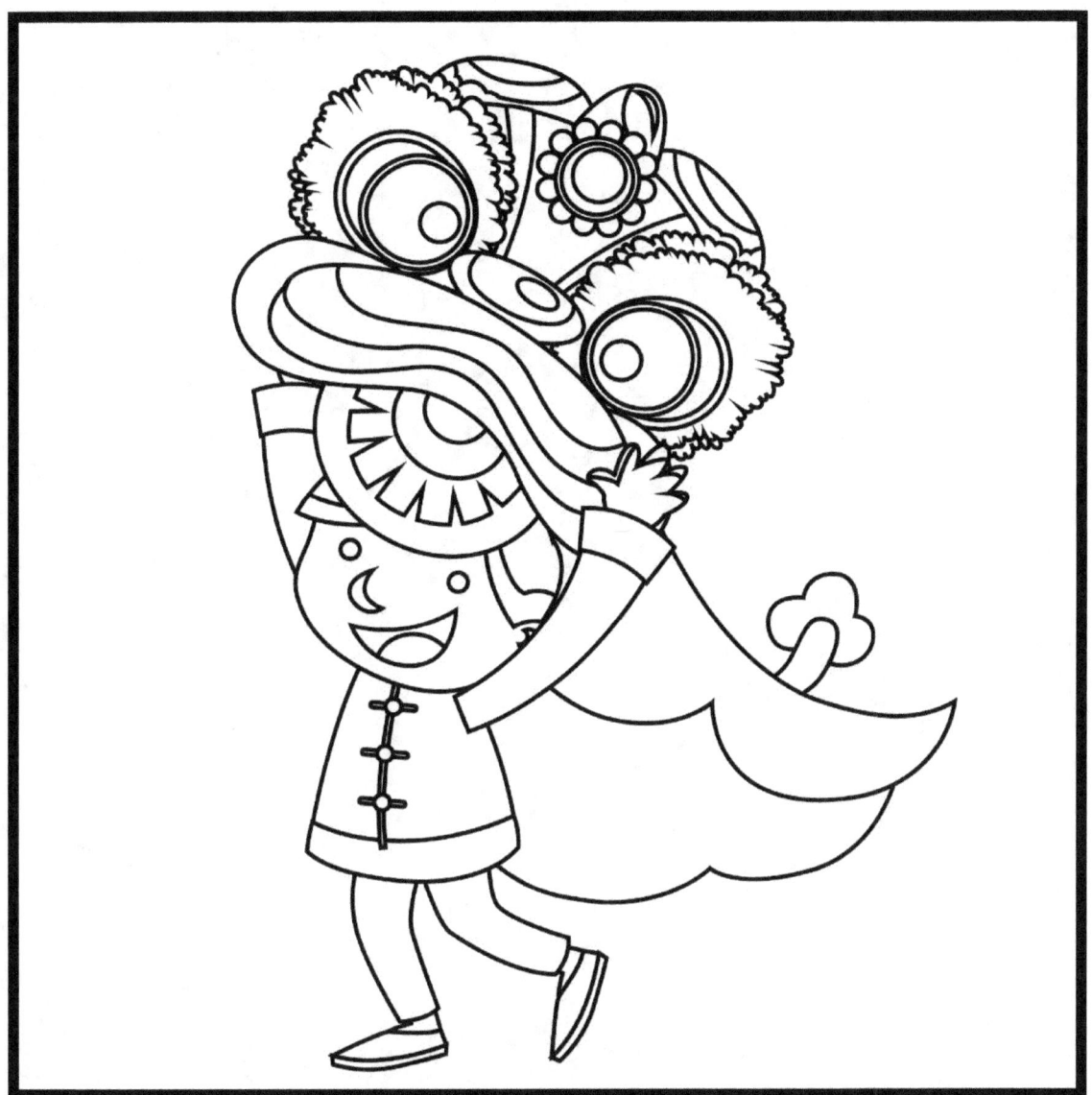

note:

_____

_____

_____

MARCH 15TH

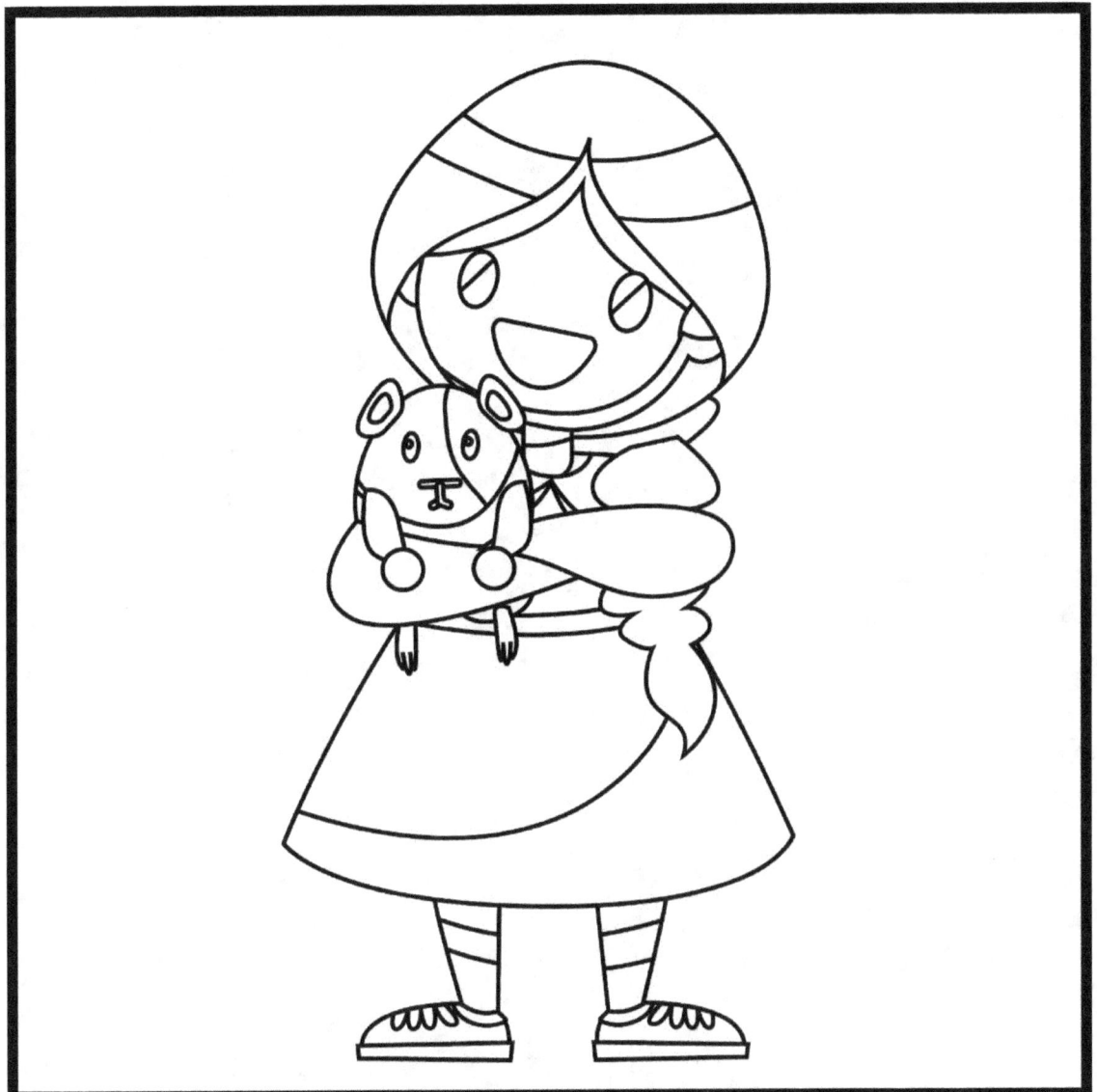

note:

_____

_____

_____

MARCH 16TH

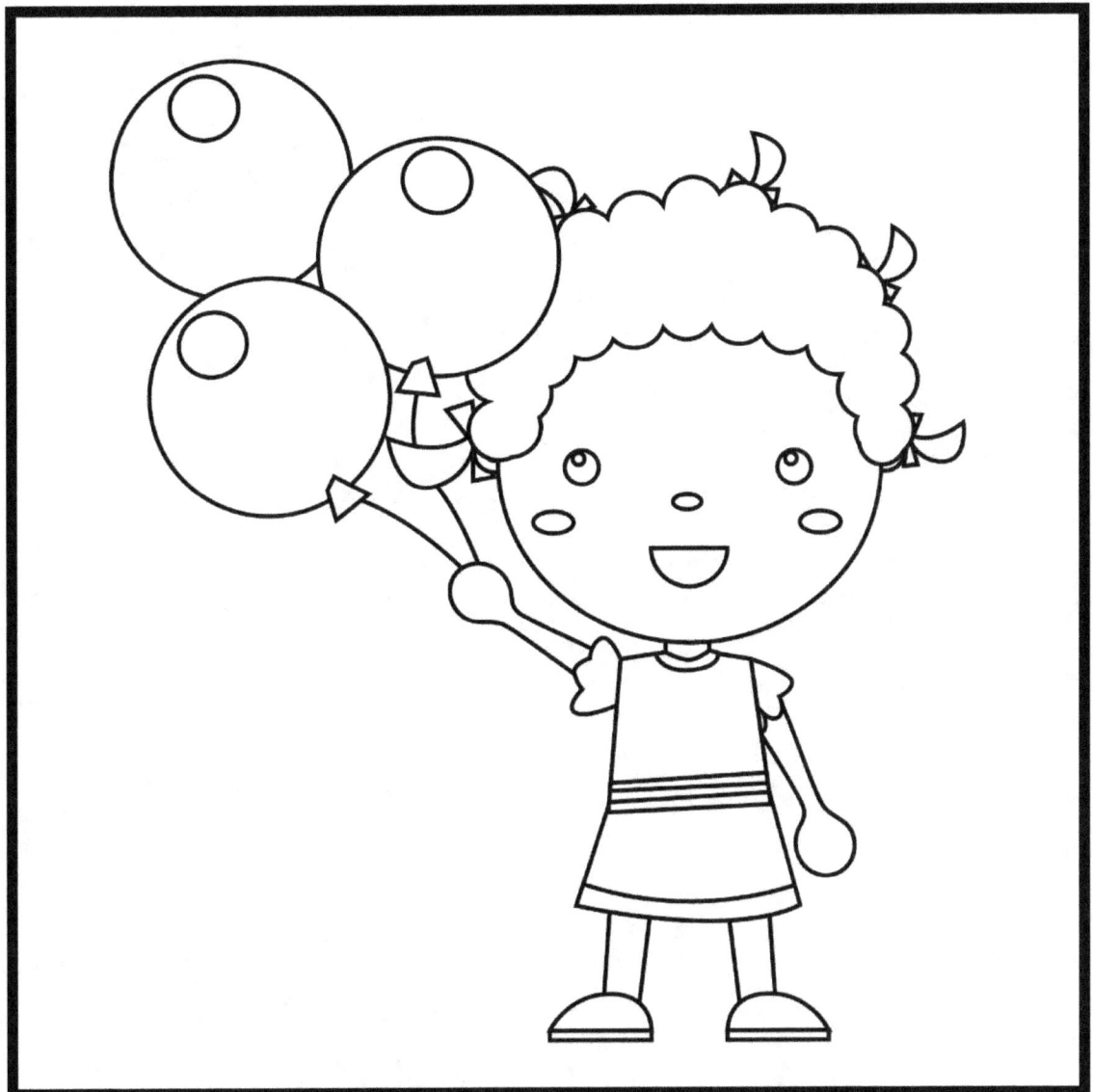

note:

_____

_____

_____

MARCH 17TH

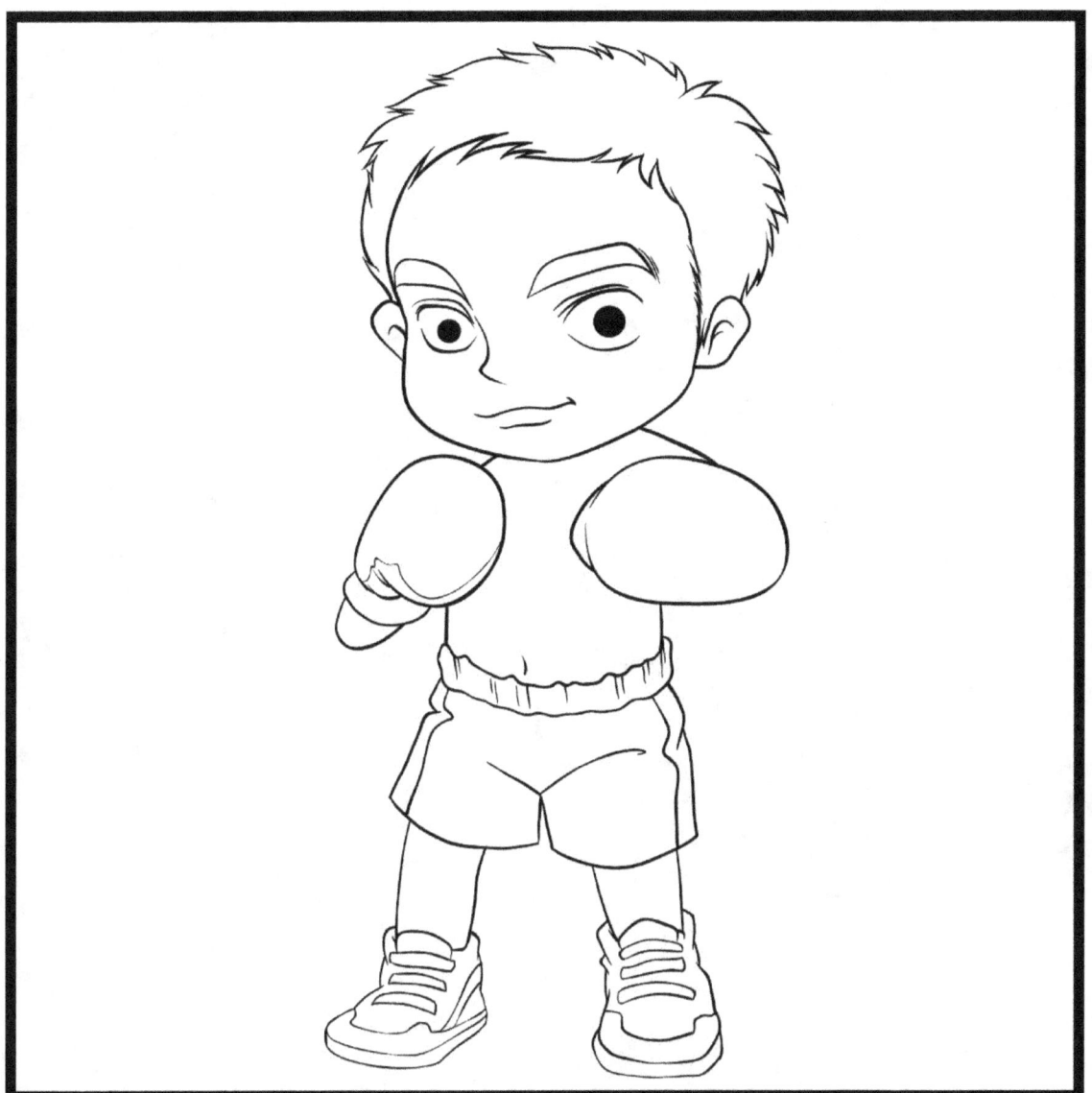

note:

_____

_____

_____

MARCH 18TH

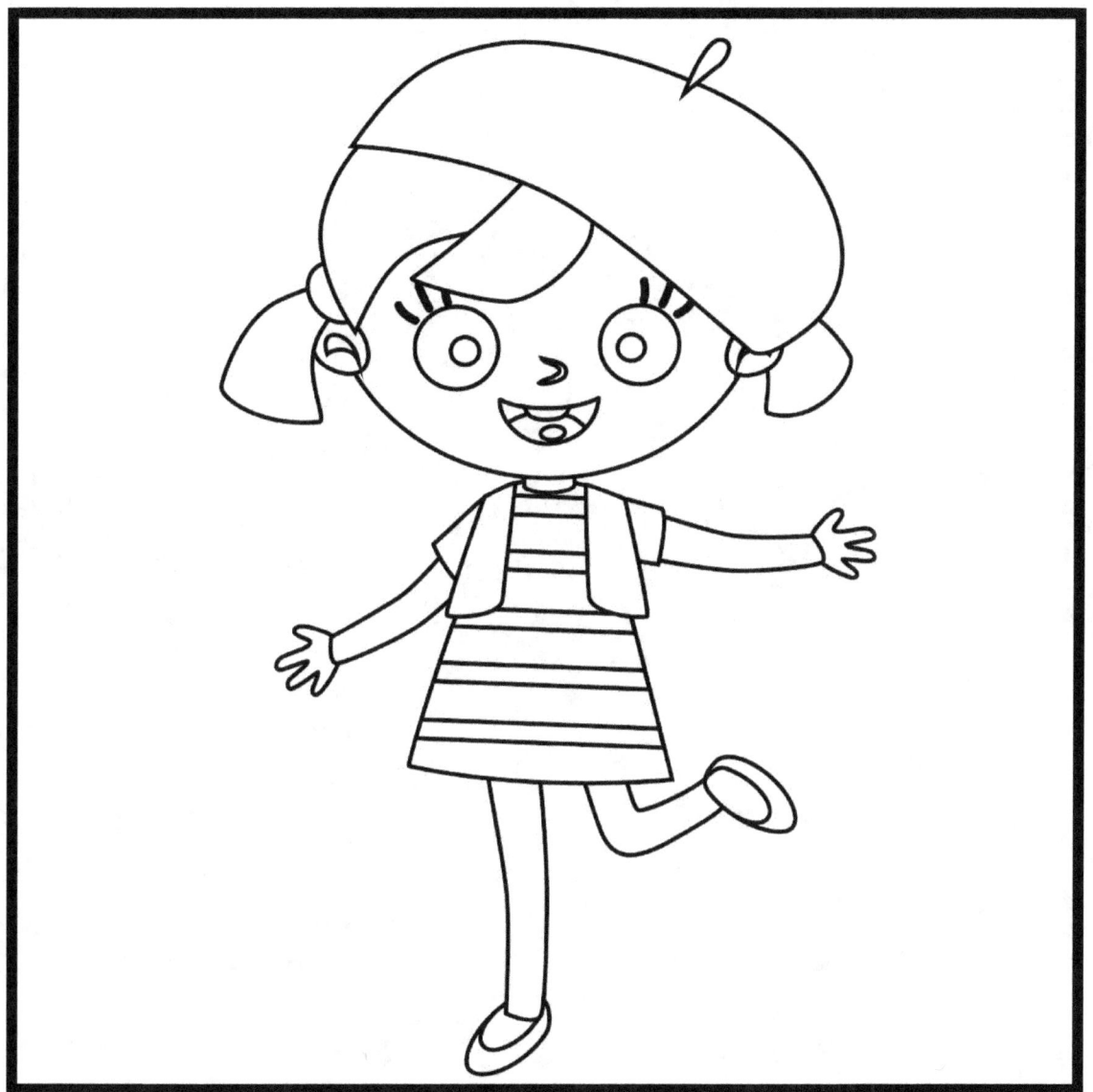

note:

_____

_____

_____

MARCH 19TH

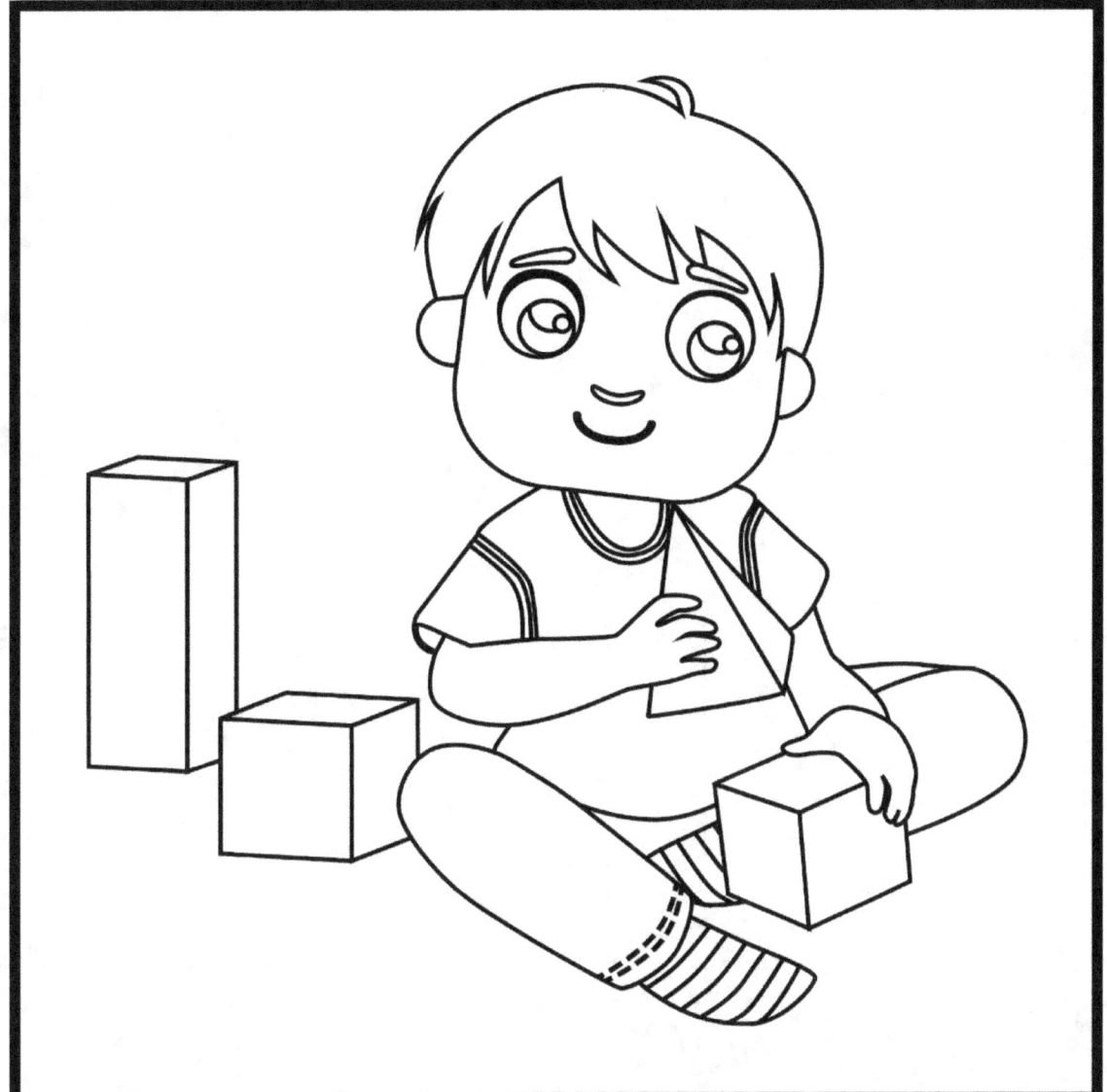

note:

_____

_____

_____

MARCH 20TH

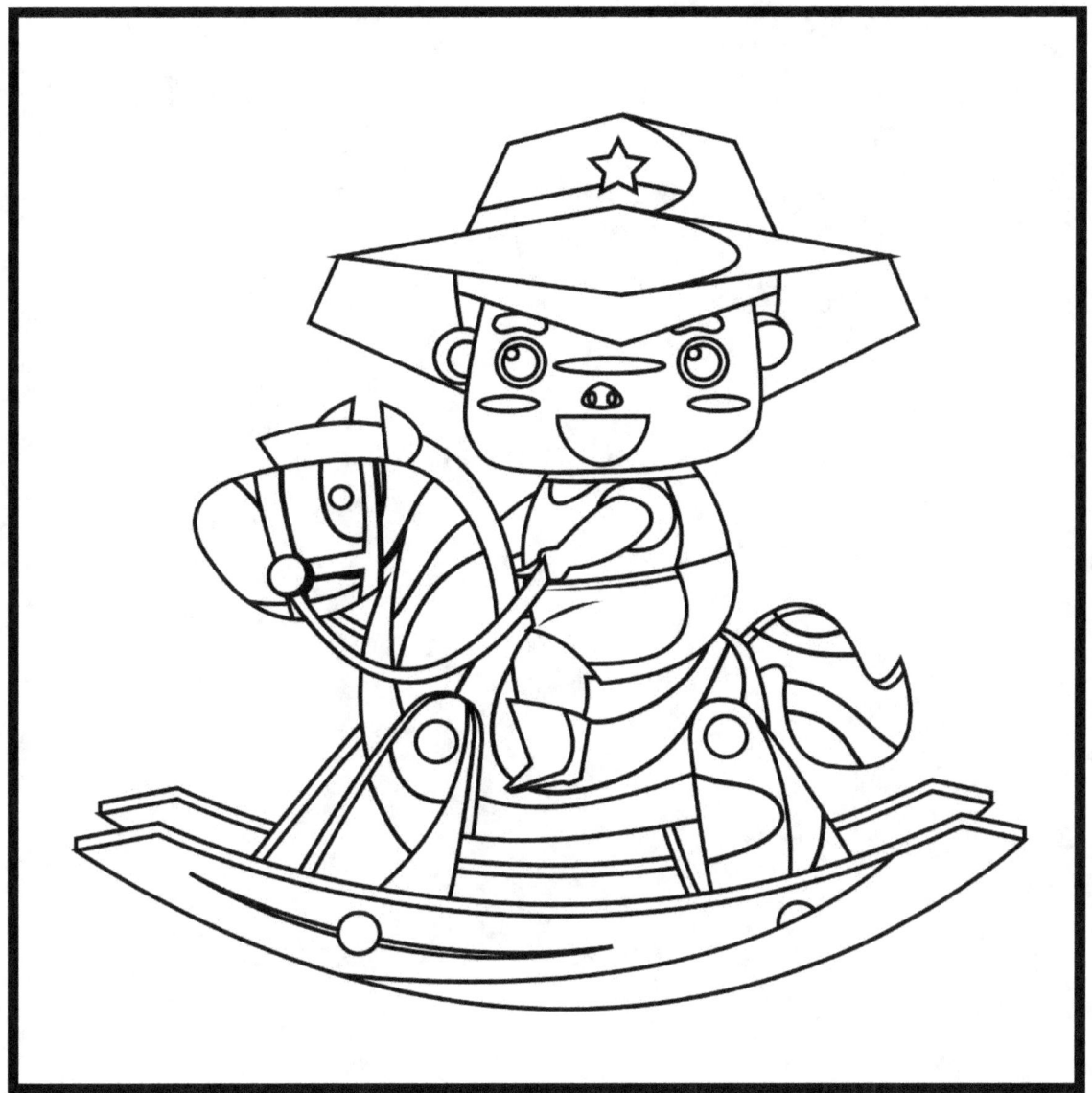

note:

_____

_____

_____

MARCH 21TH

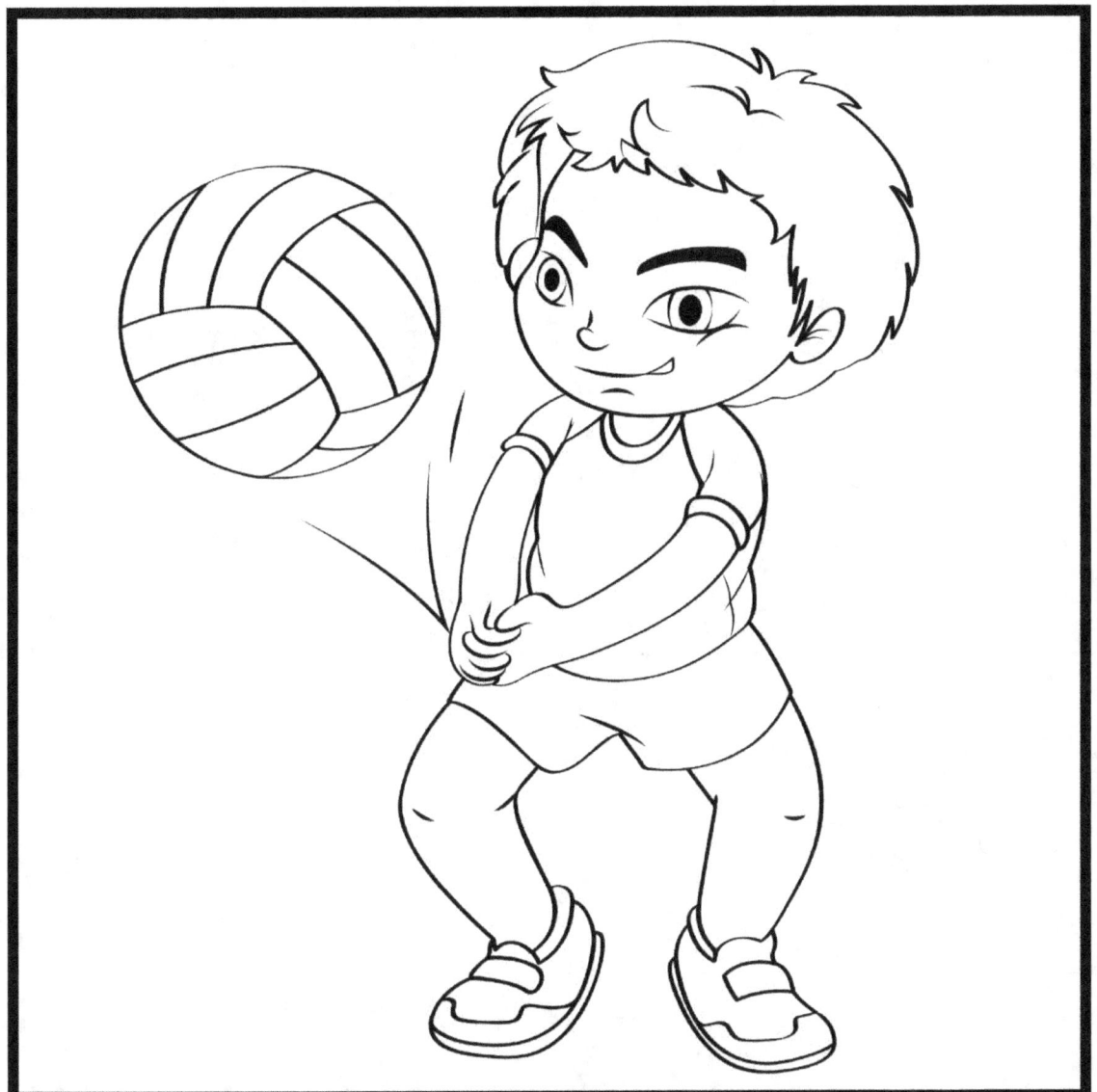

note:

_____

_____

_____

MARCH 22TH

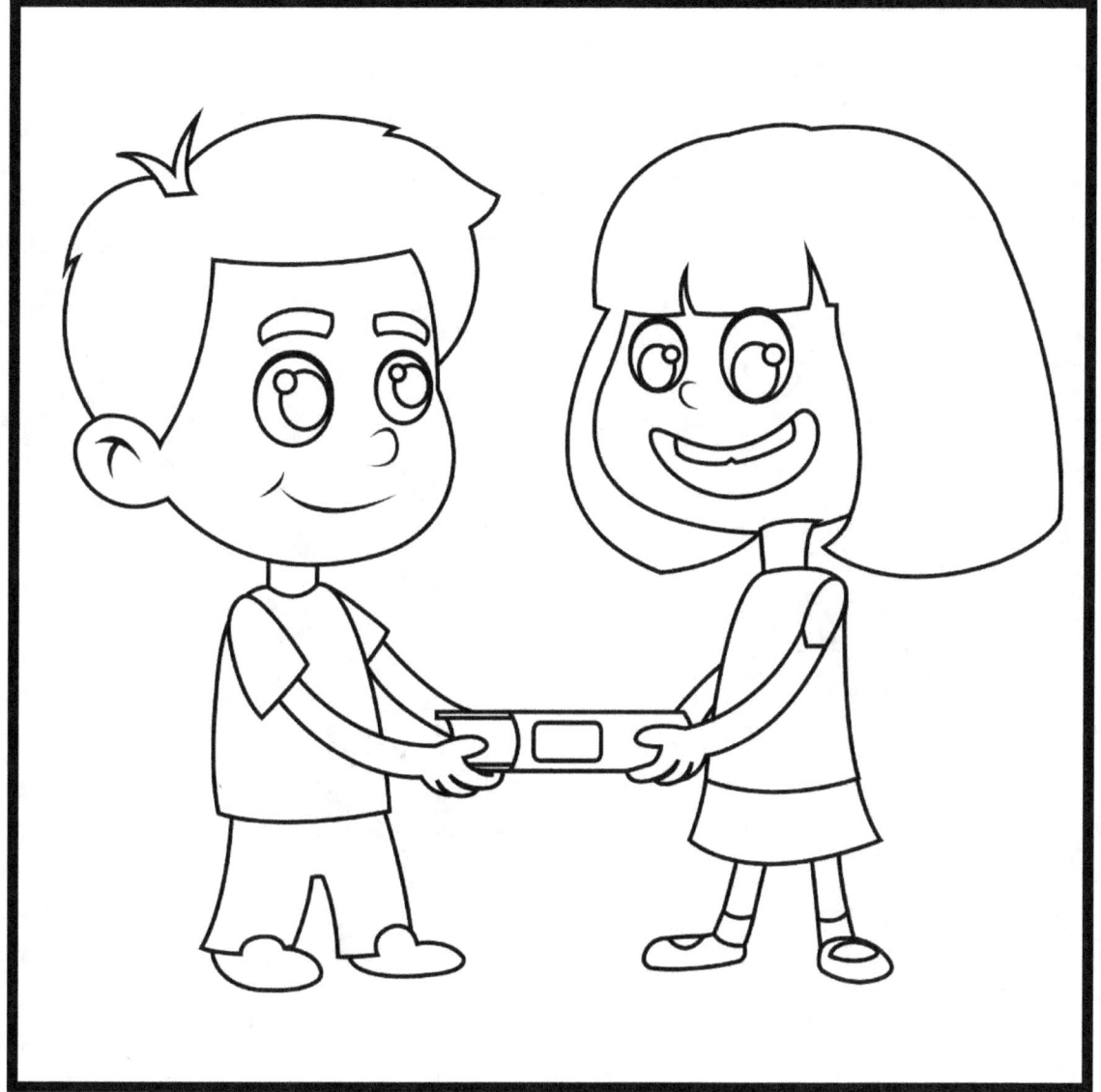

note:

_____

_____

_____

MARCH 23TH

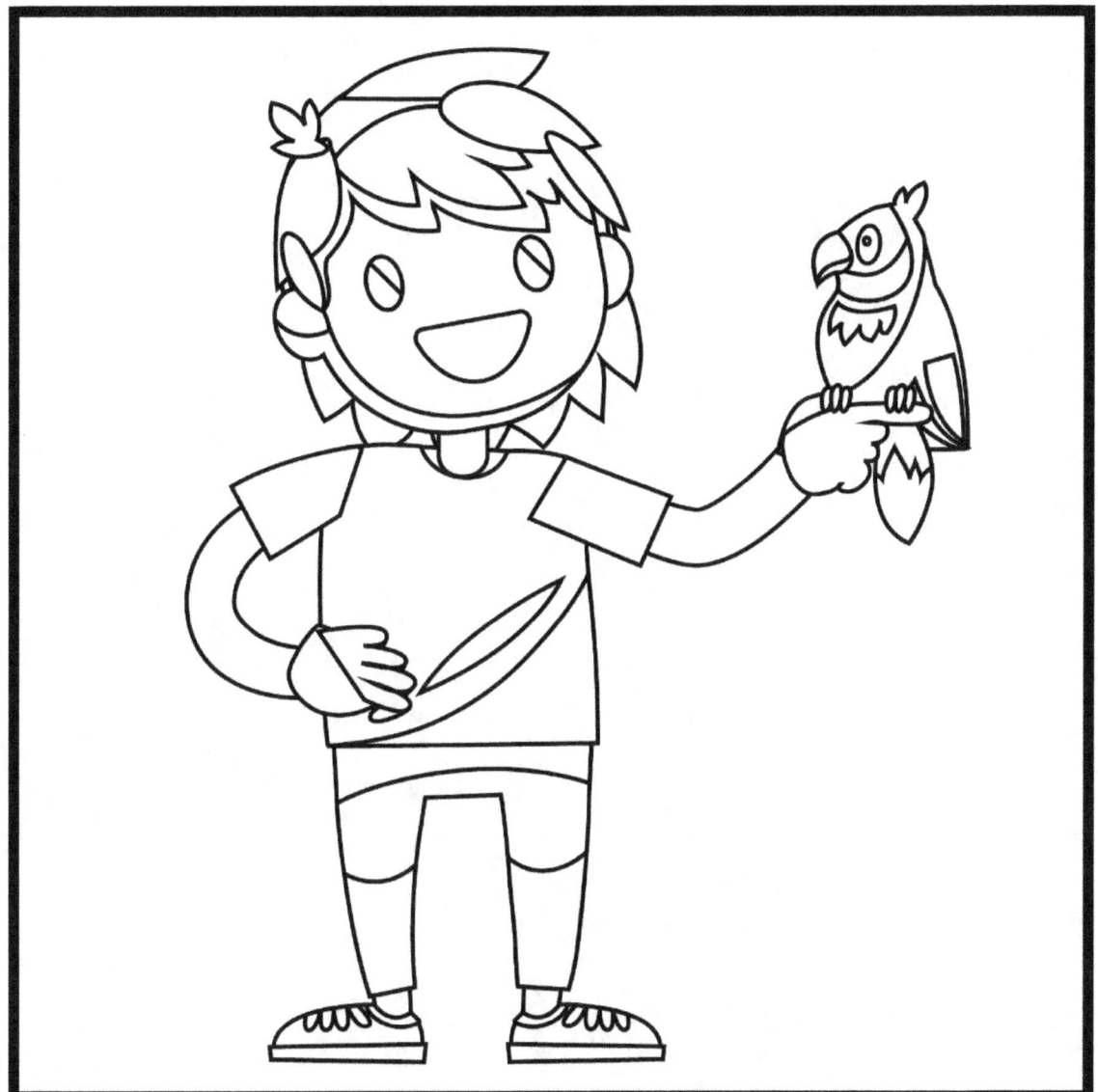

note:

_____

_____

_____

MARCH 24TH

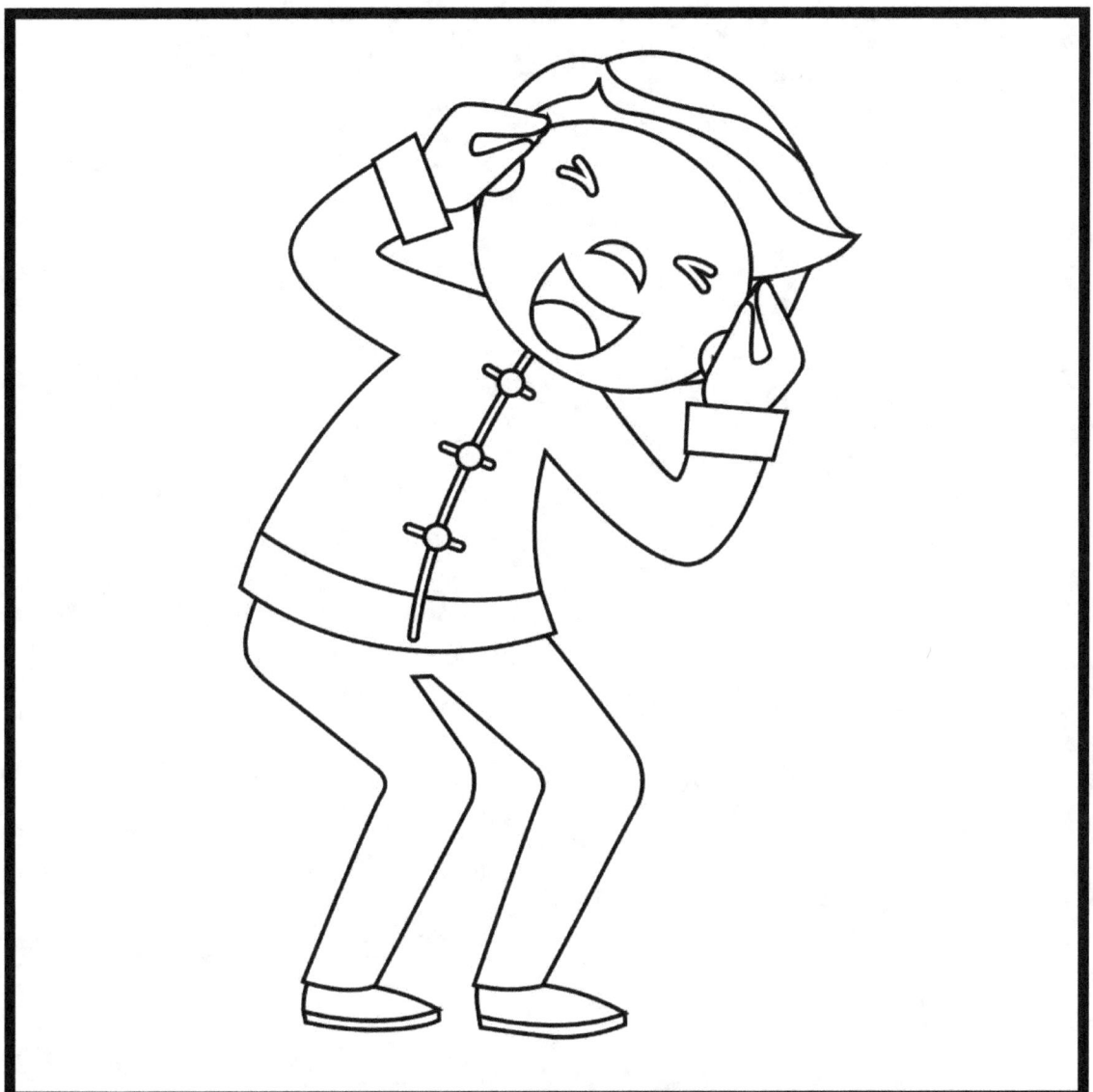

note:

_____

_____

_____

MARCH 25TH

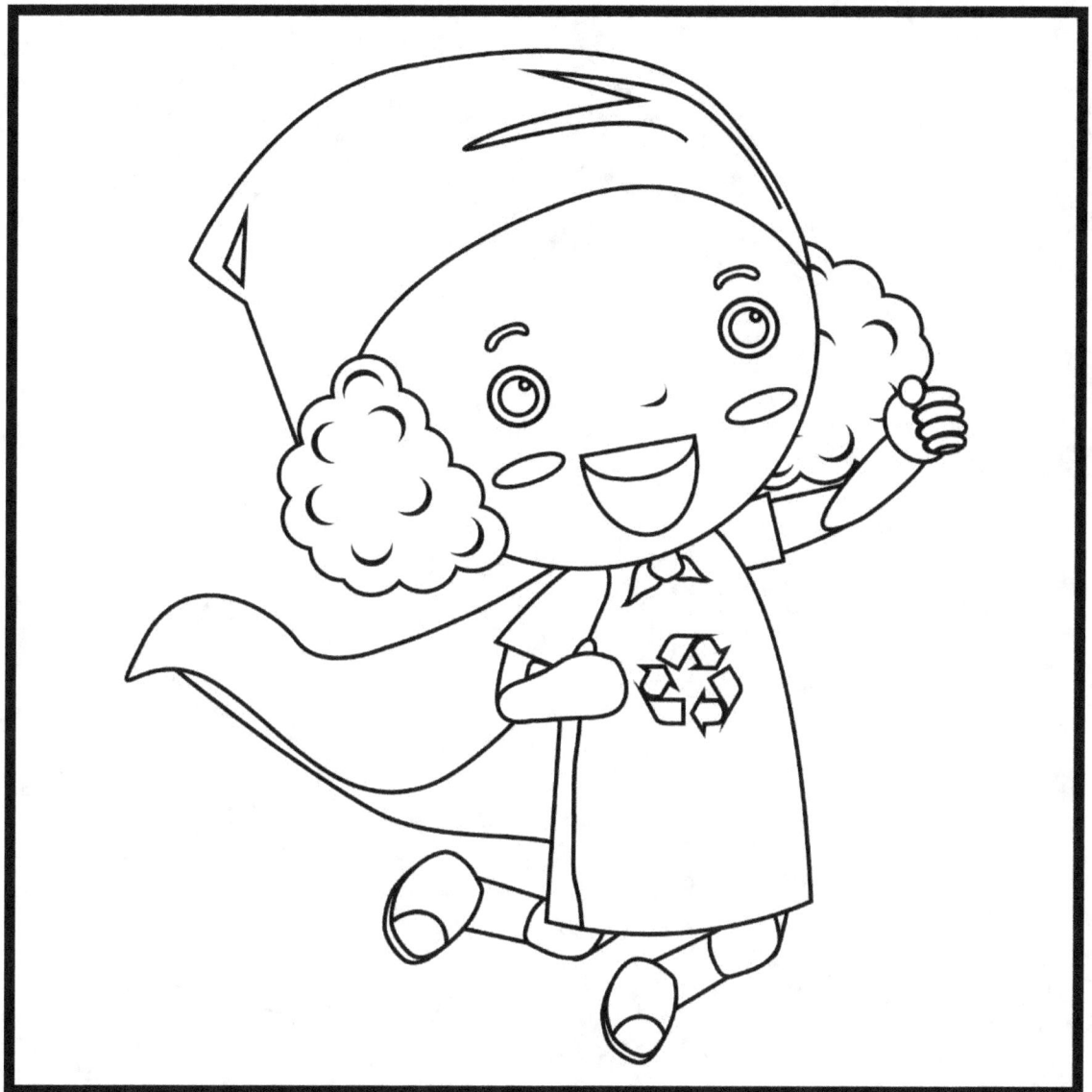

note:

_____

_____

_____

MARCH 26TH

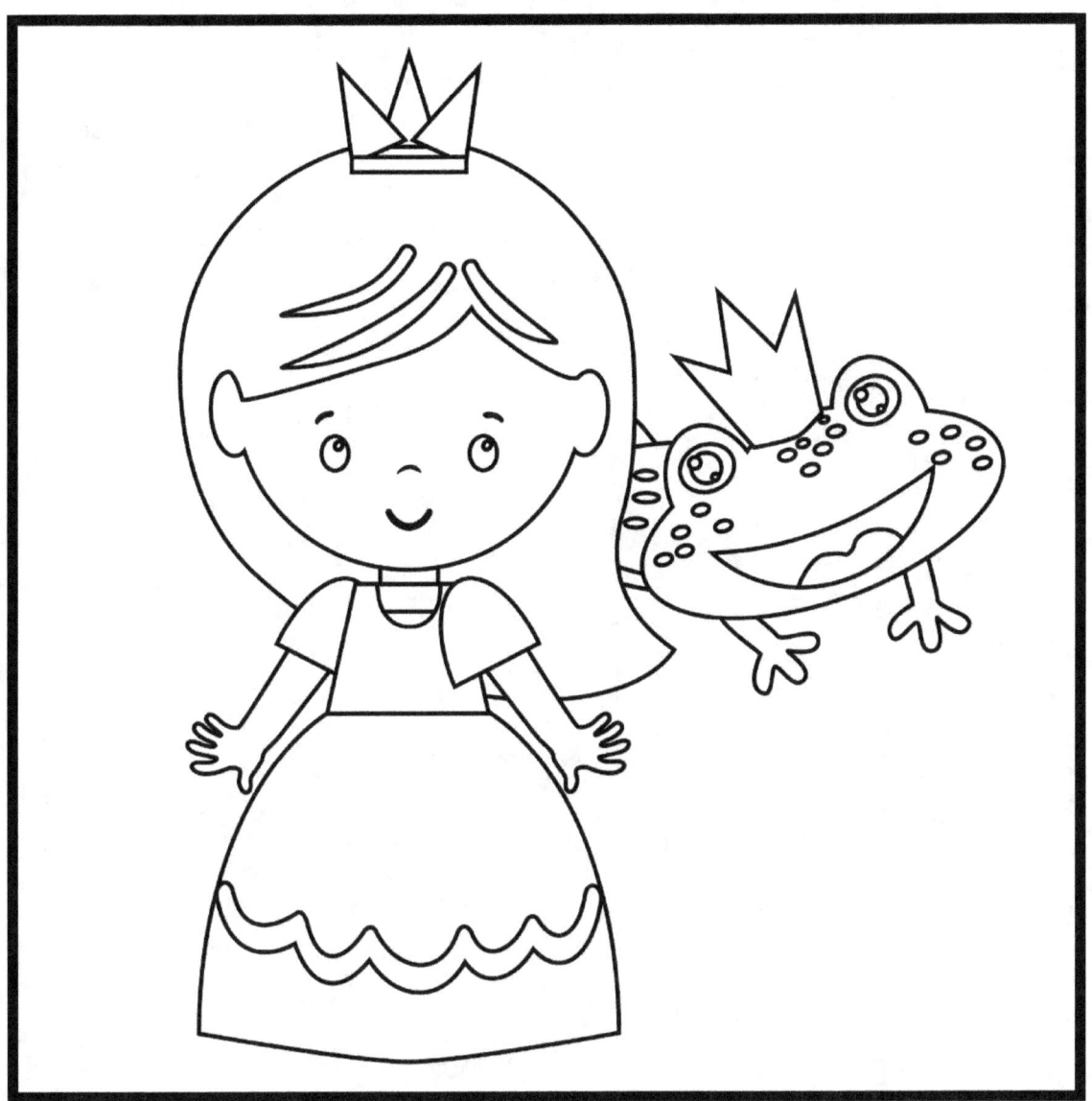

note:

_____

_____

_____

MARCH 27TH

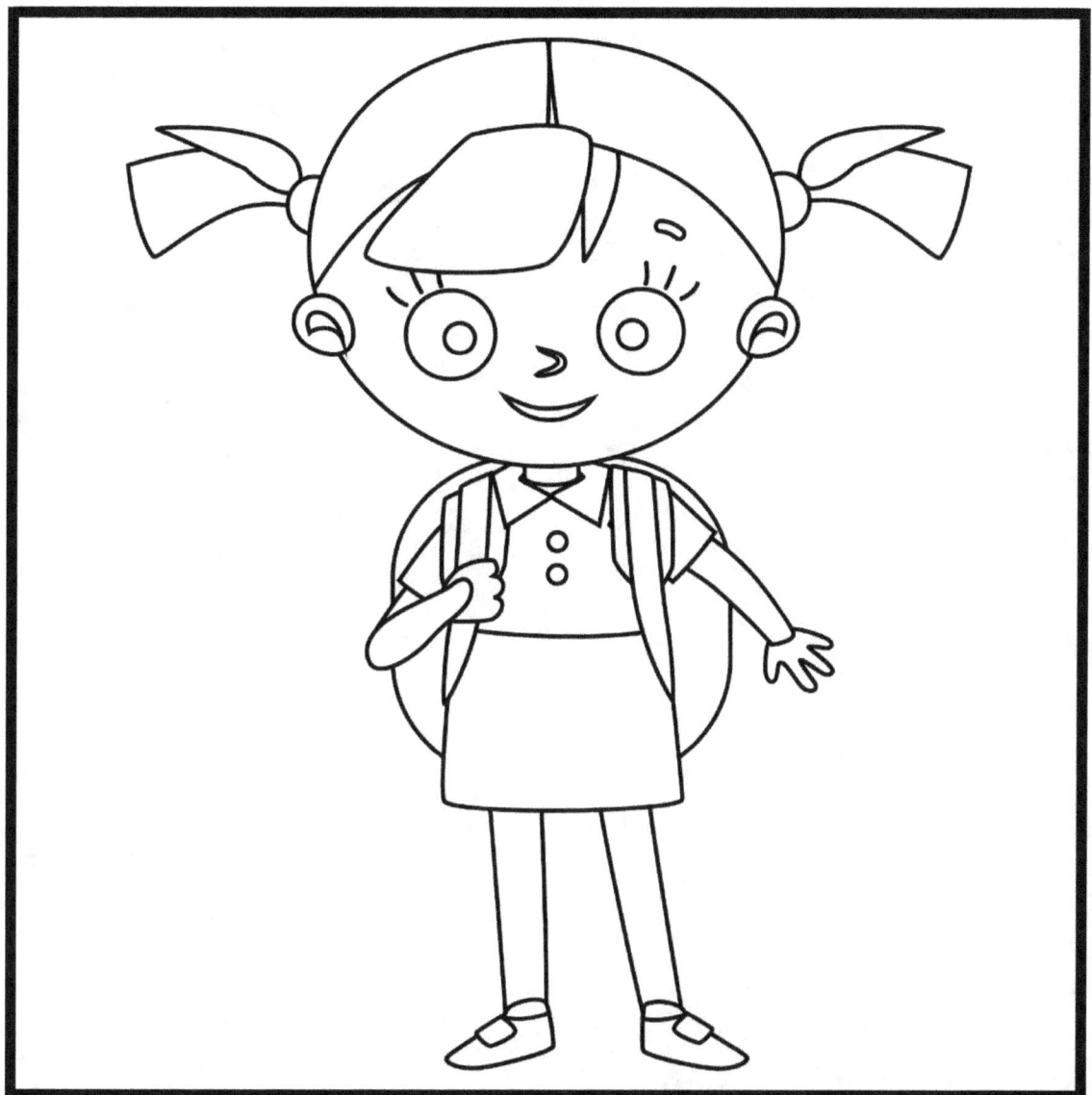

note:

_____

_____

_____

MARCH 28TH

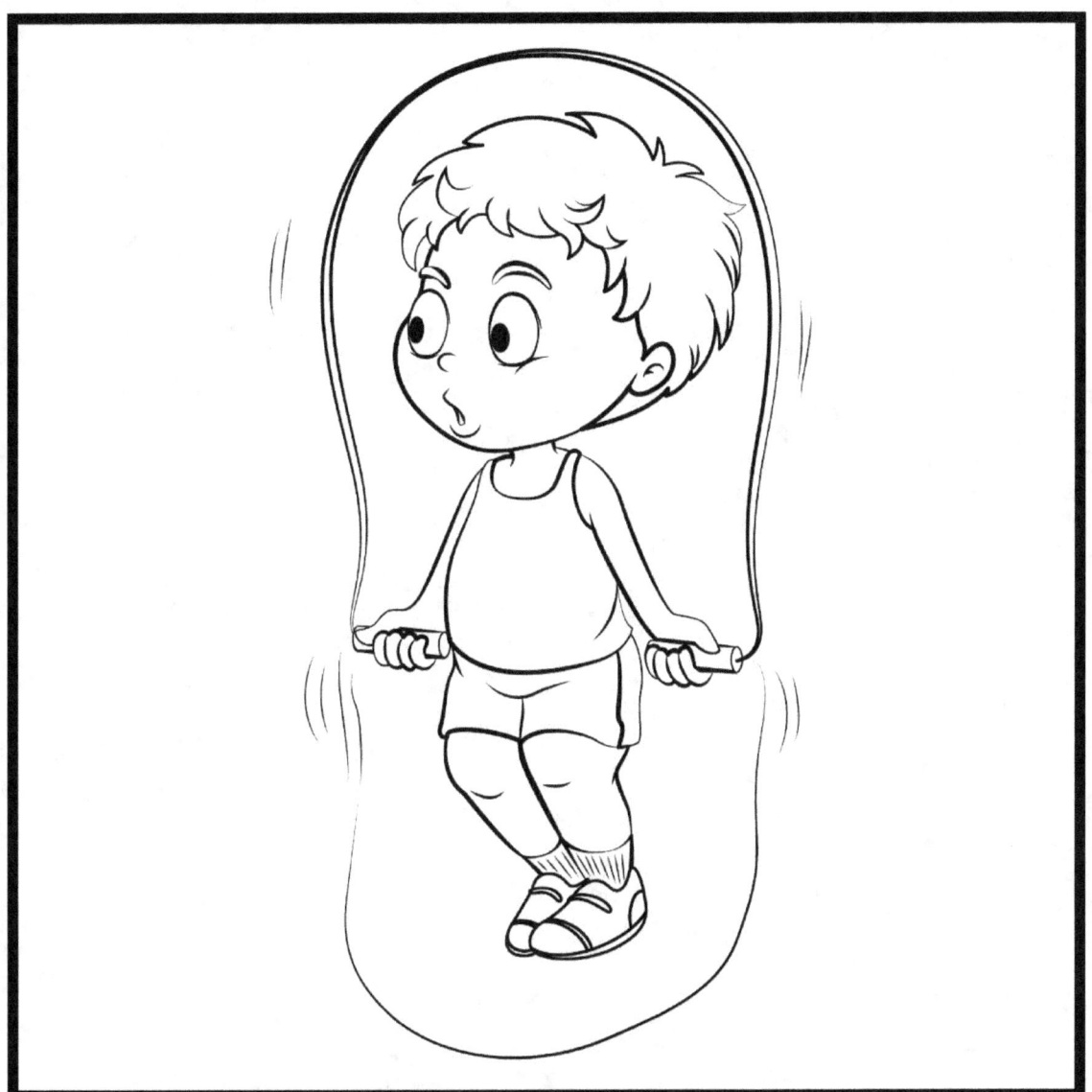

note:

_____

_____

_____

MARCH 29TH

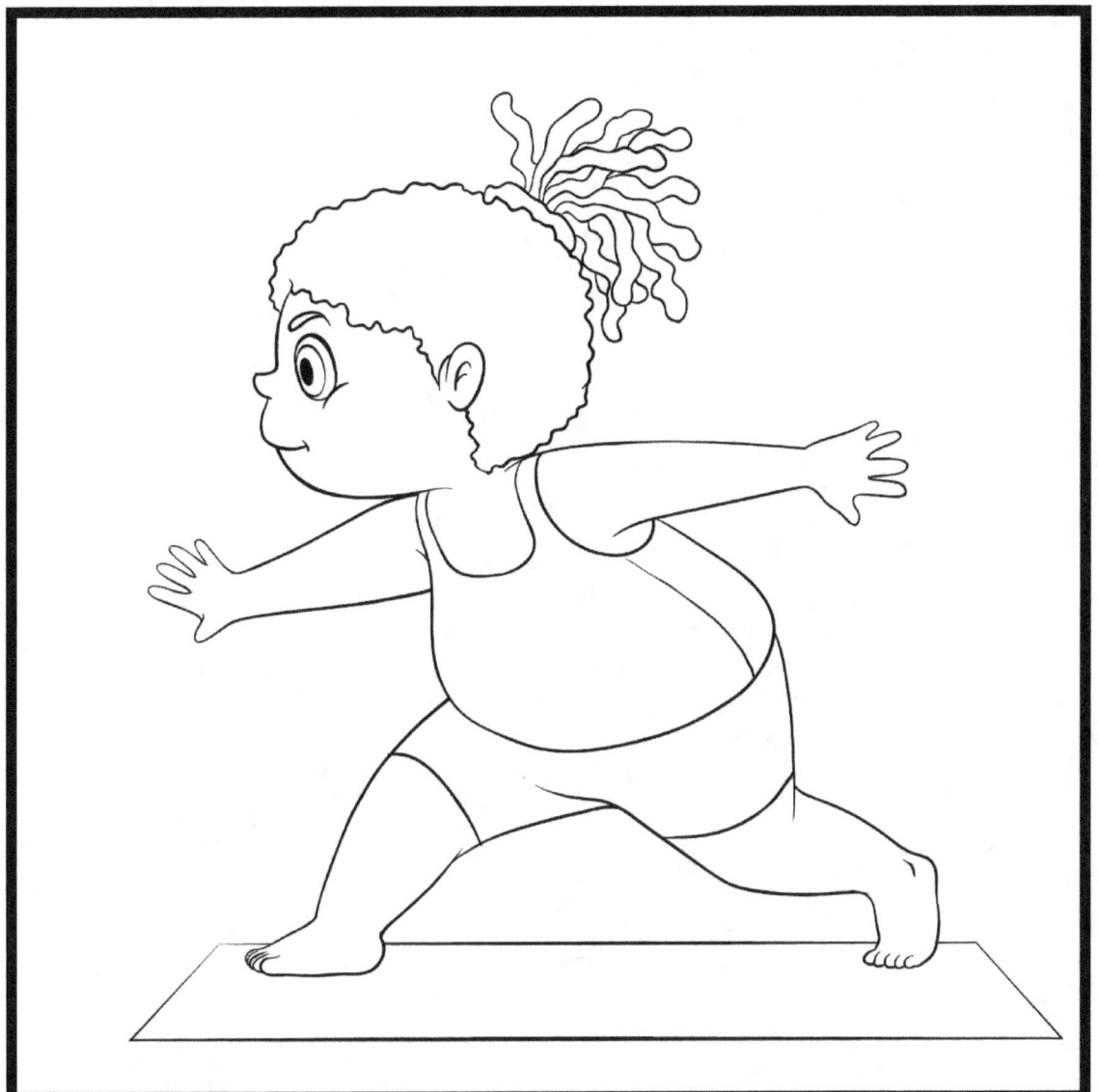

note:

_____

_____

_____

MARCH 30TH

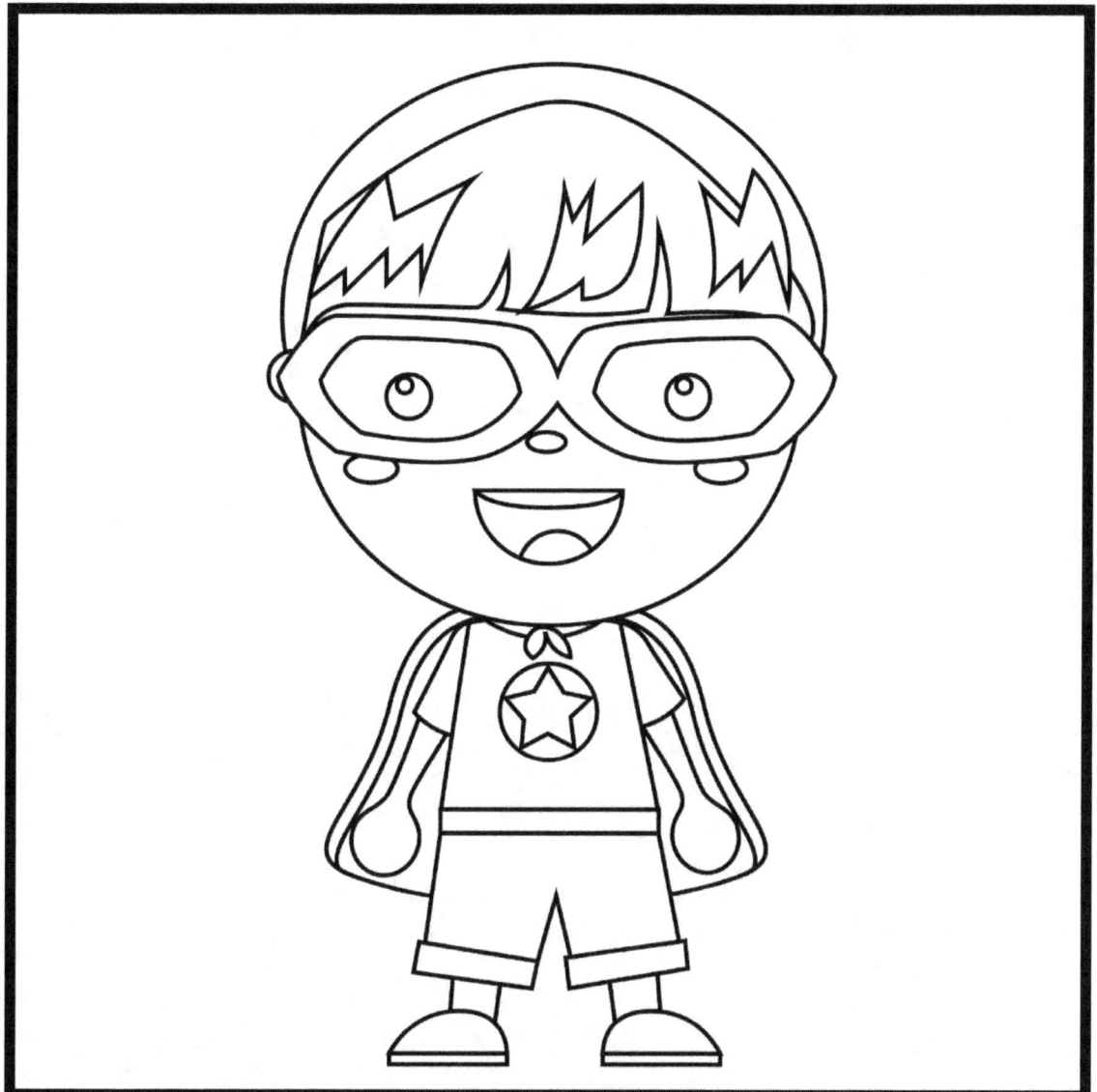

note:

_____

_____

_____

MARCH 31TH

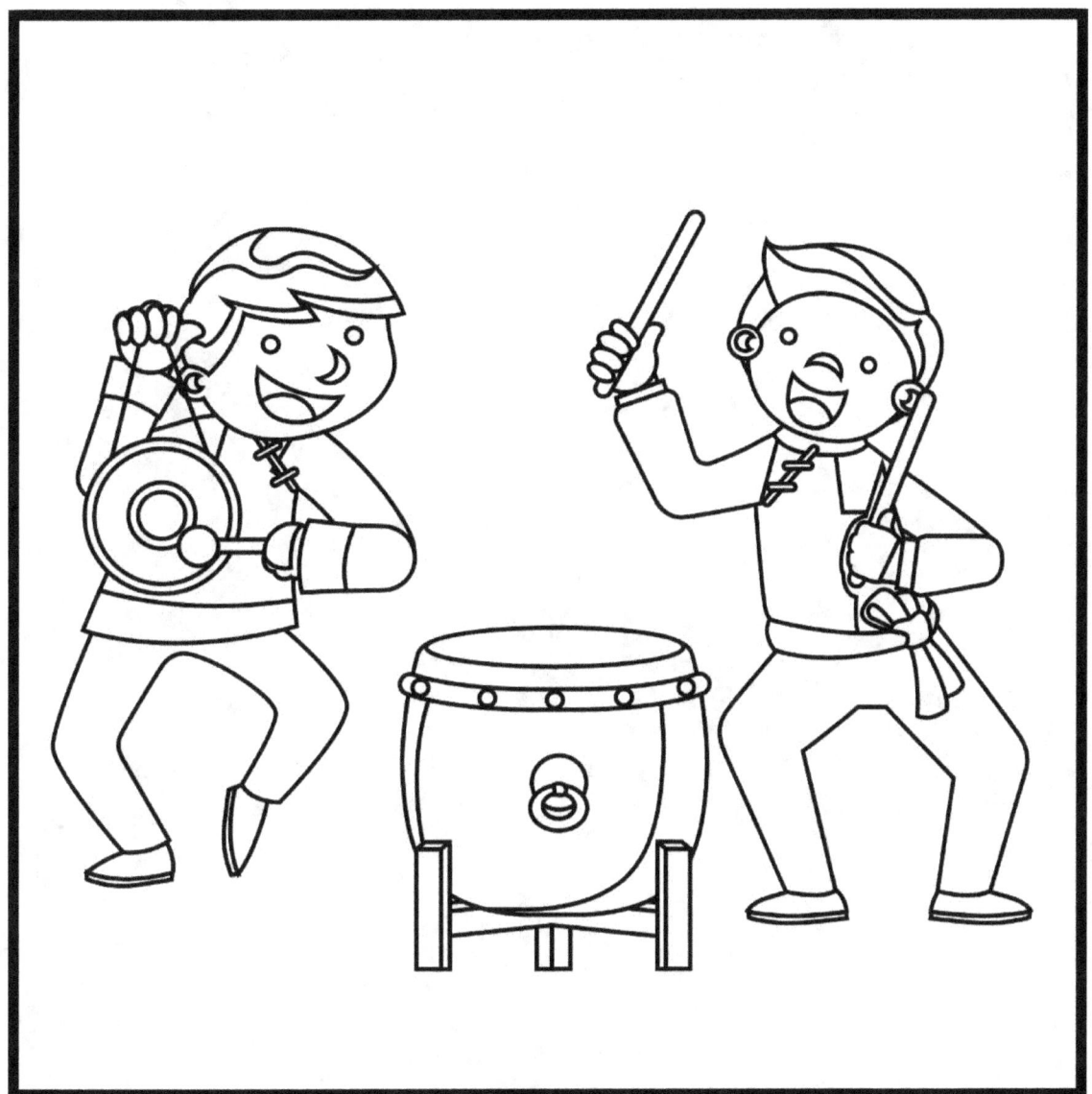

note:

_____

_____

_____

MARCH 32TH

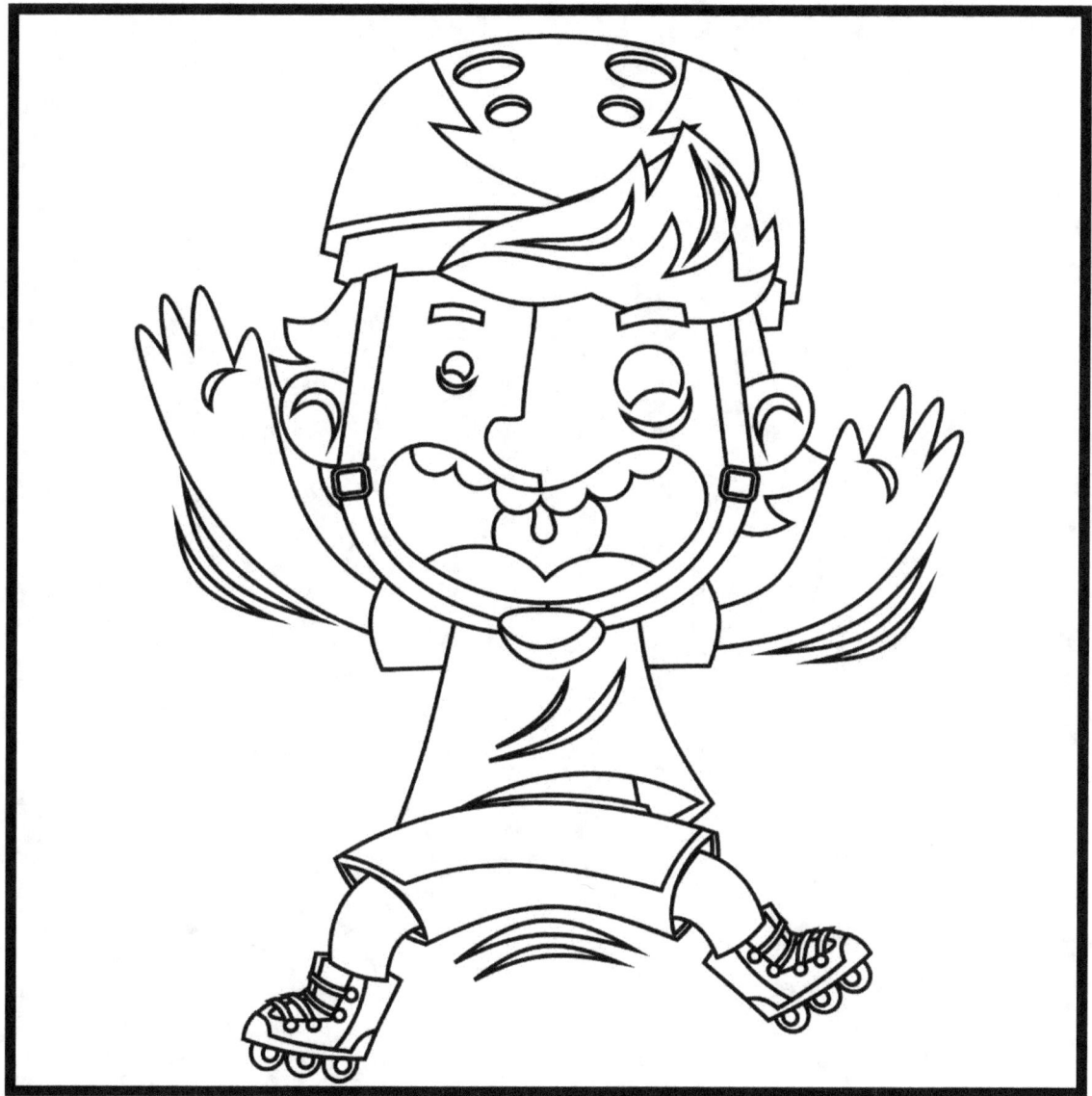

note:

_____

_____

_____

MARCH 33TH

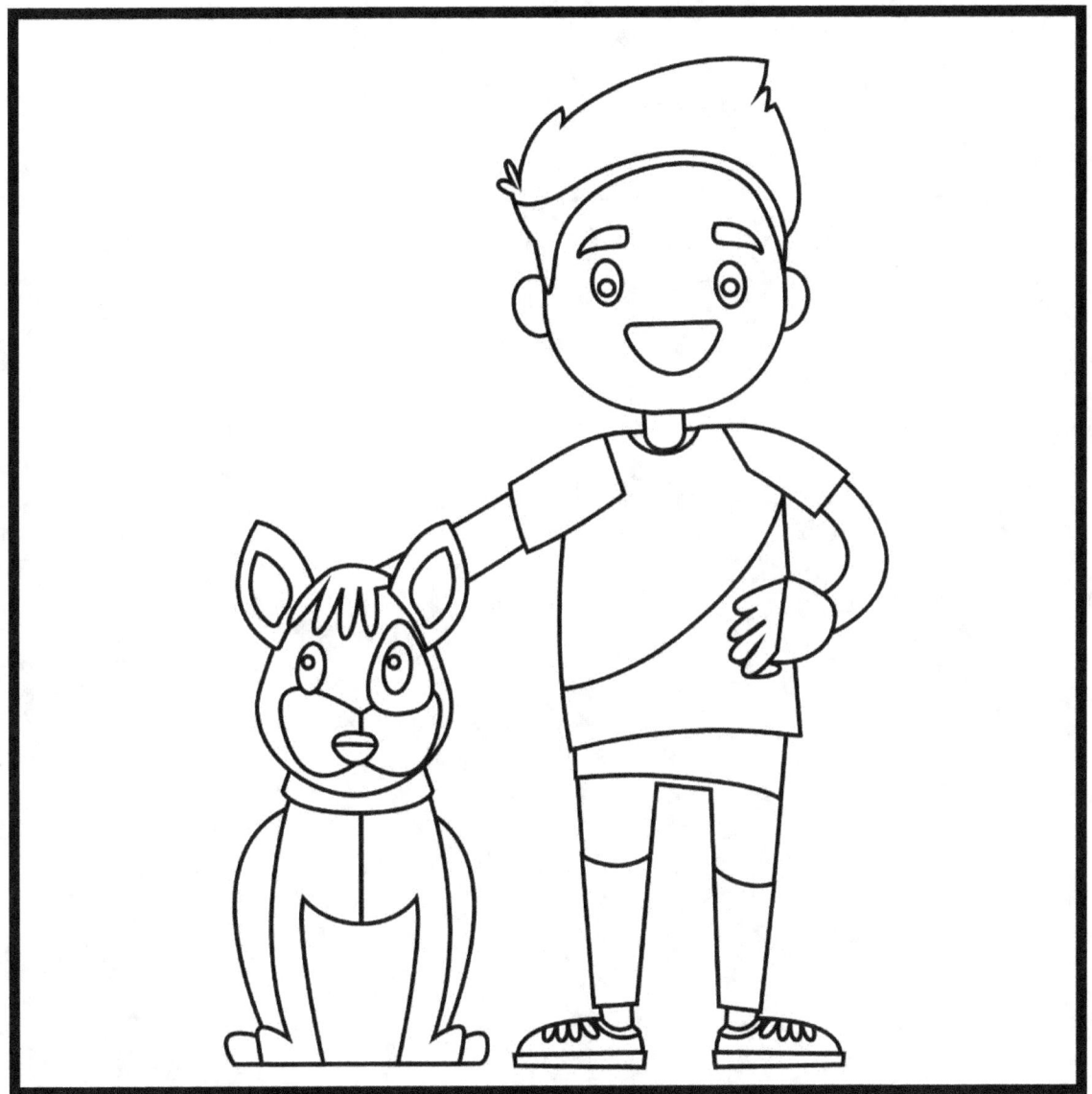

note:

_____

_____

_____

MARCH 34TH

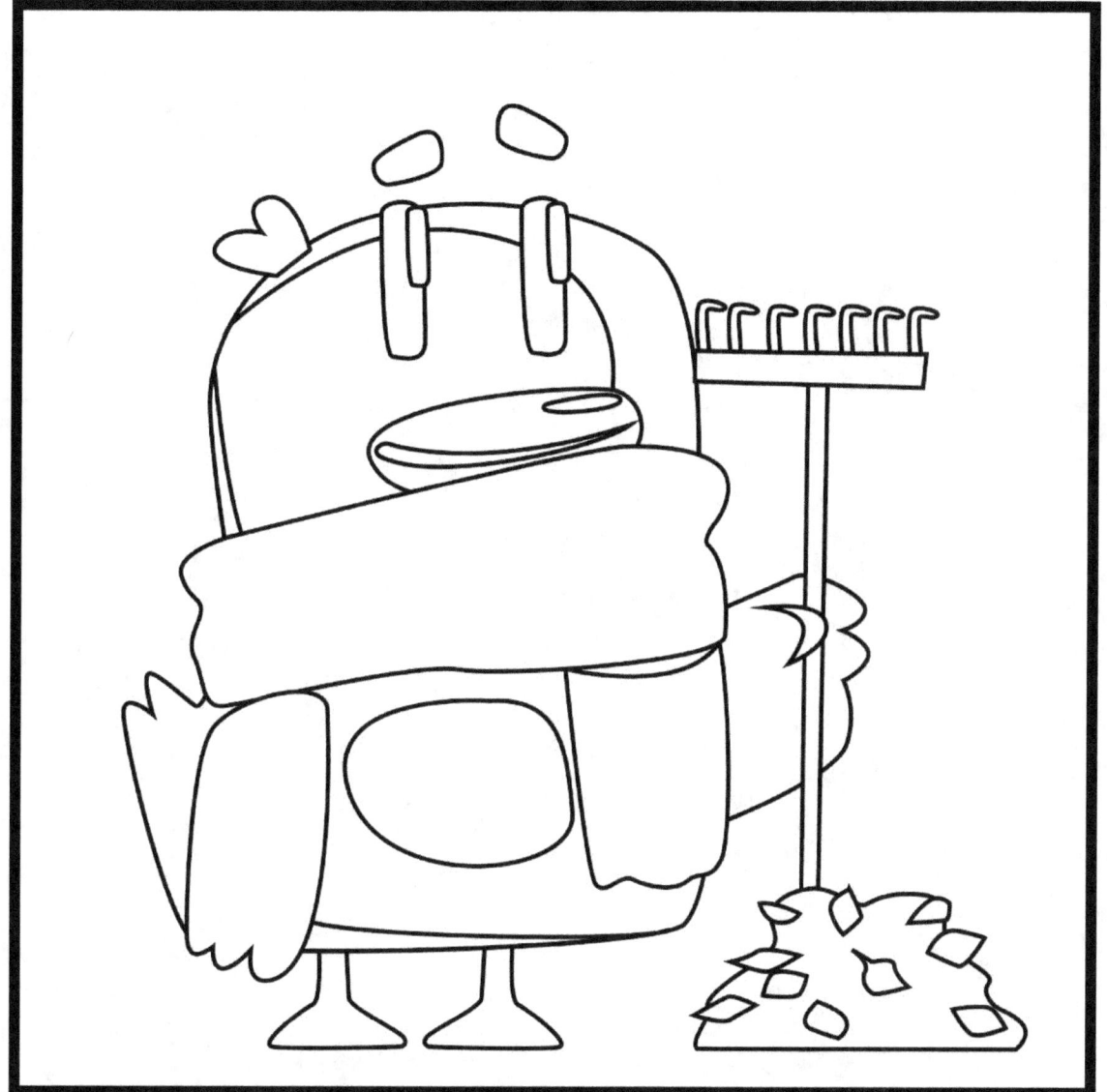

note:

_____

_____

_____

MARCH 35TH

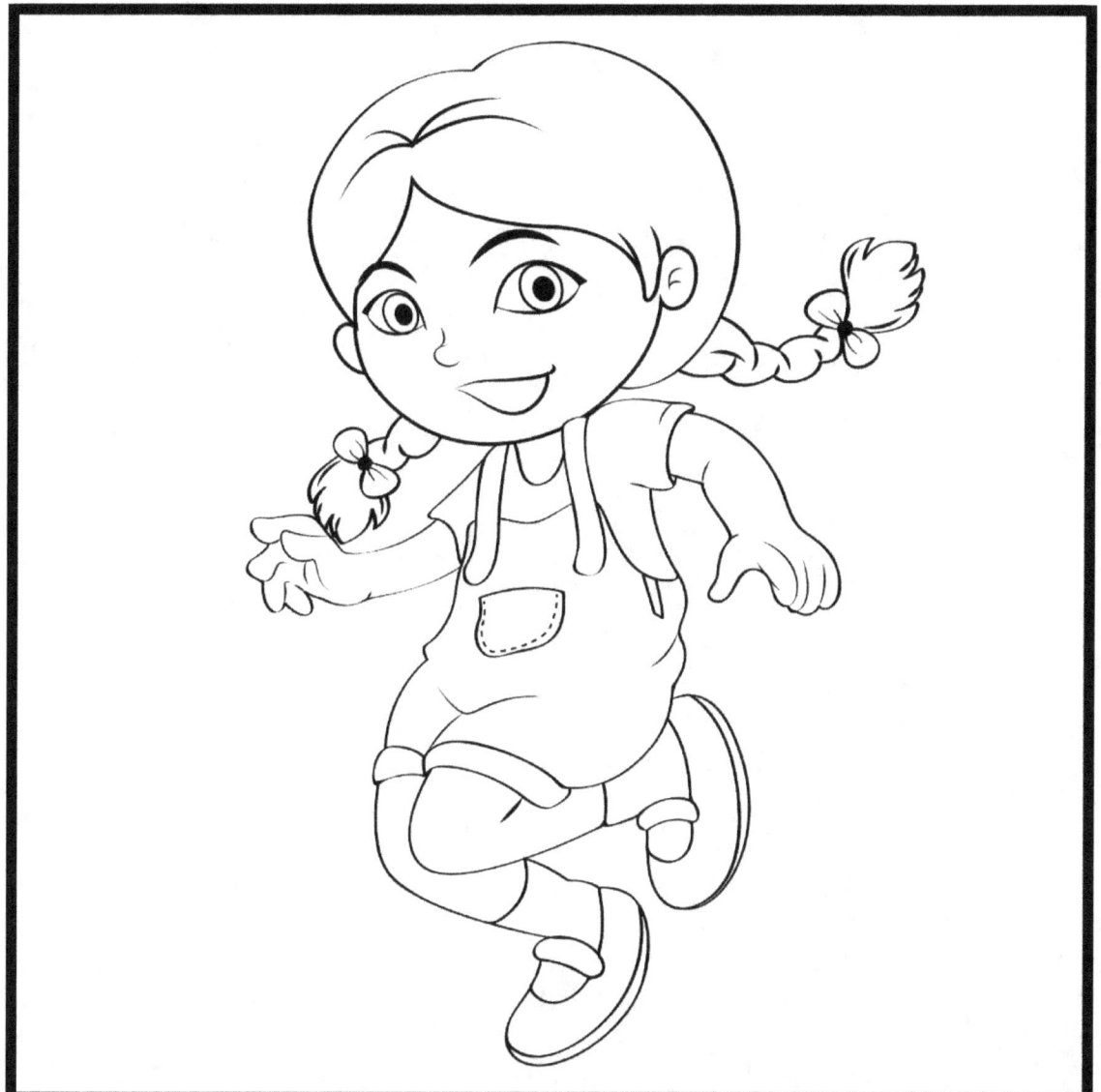

note:

_____

_____

_____

MARCH 36TH

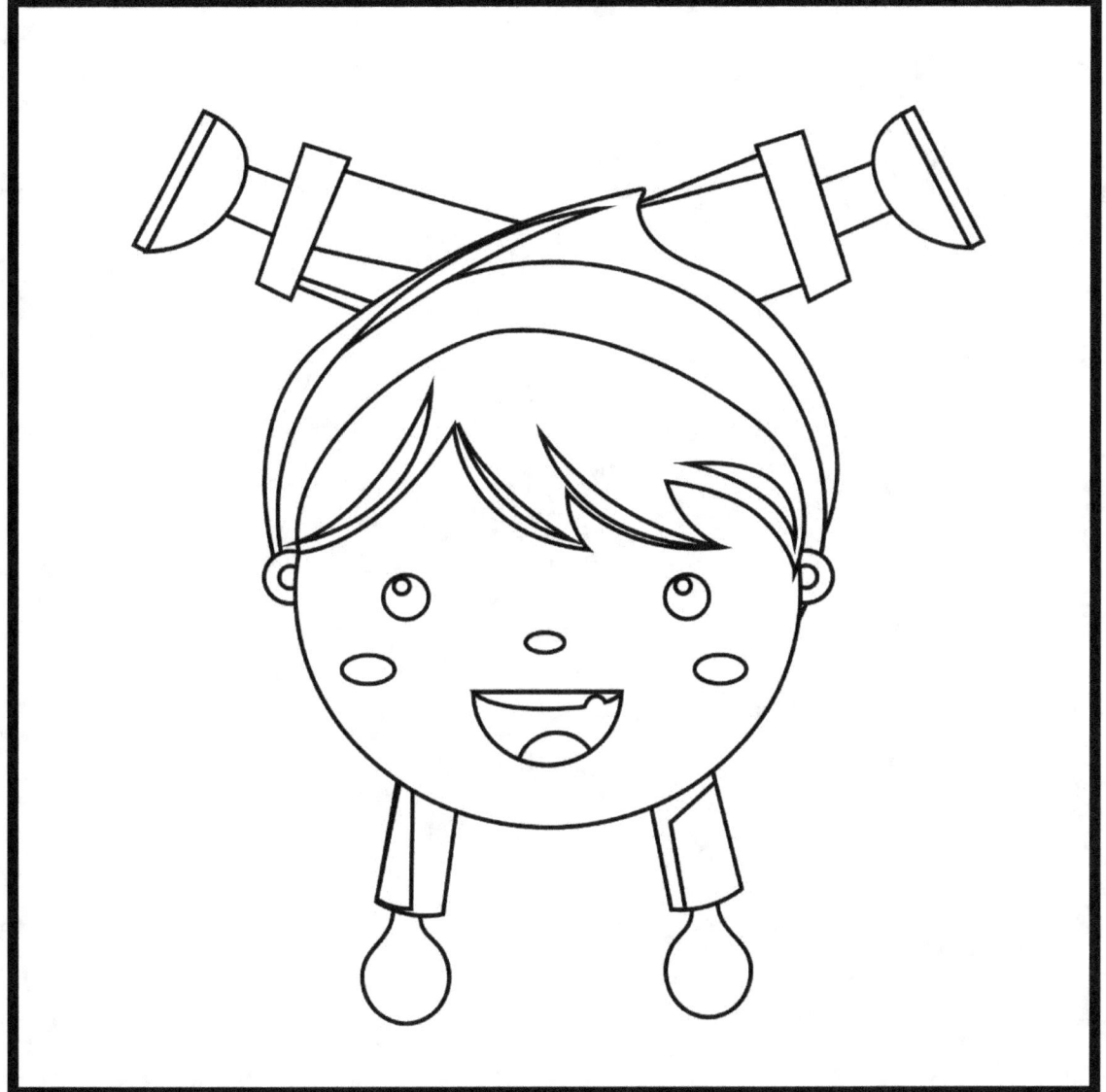

note:

_____

_____

_____

MARCH 37TH

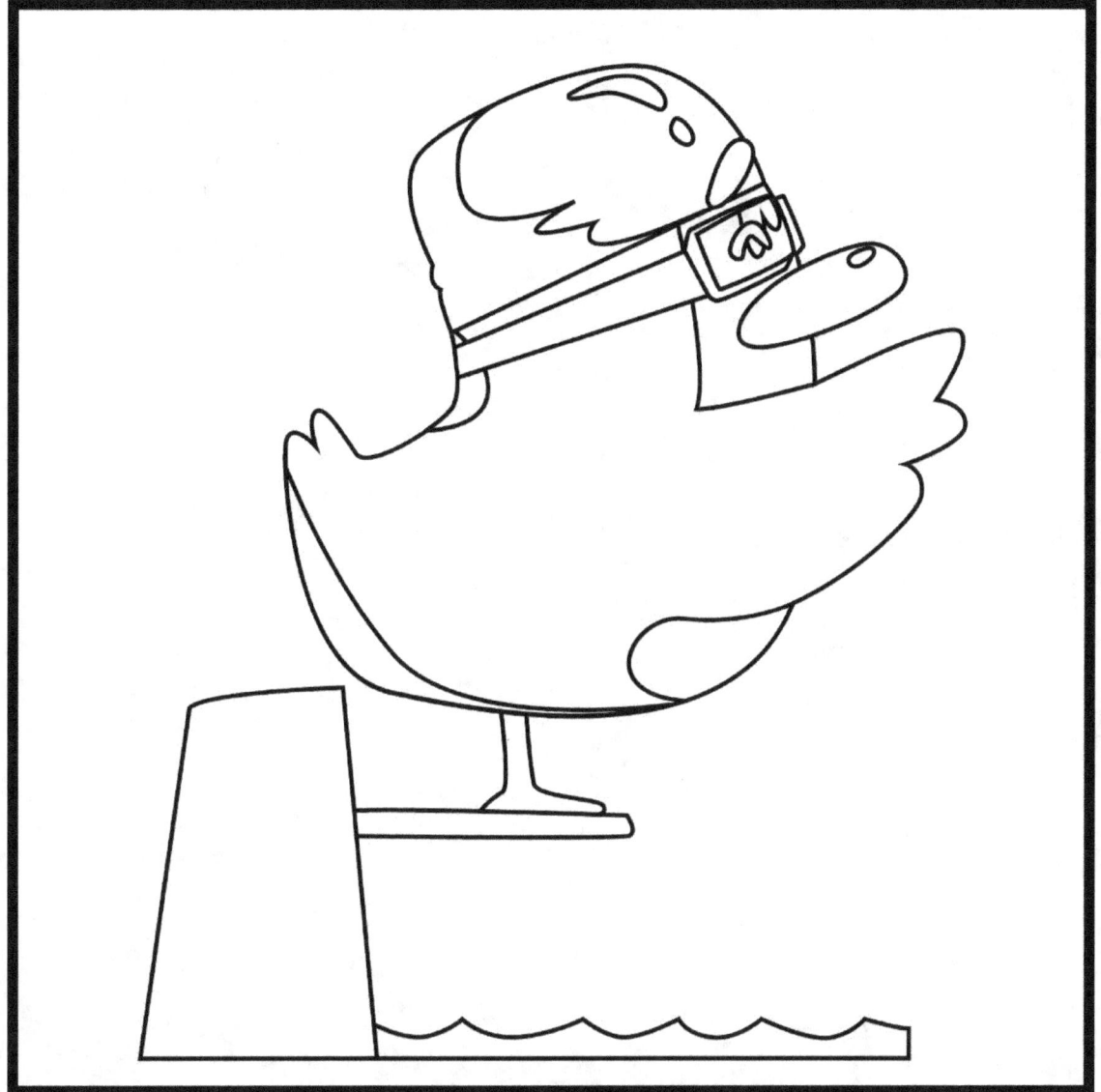

note:

_____

_____

_____

MARCH 38TH

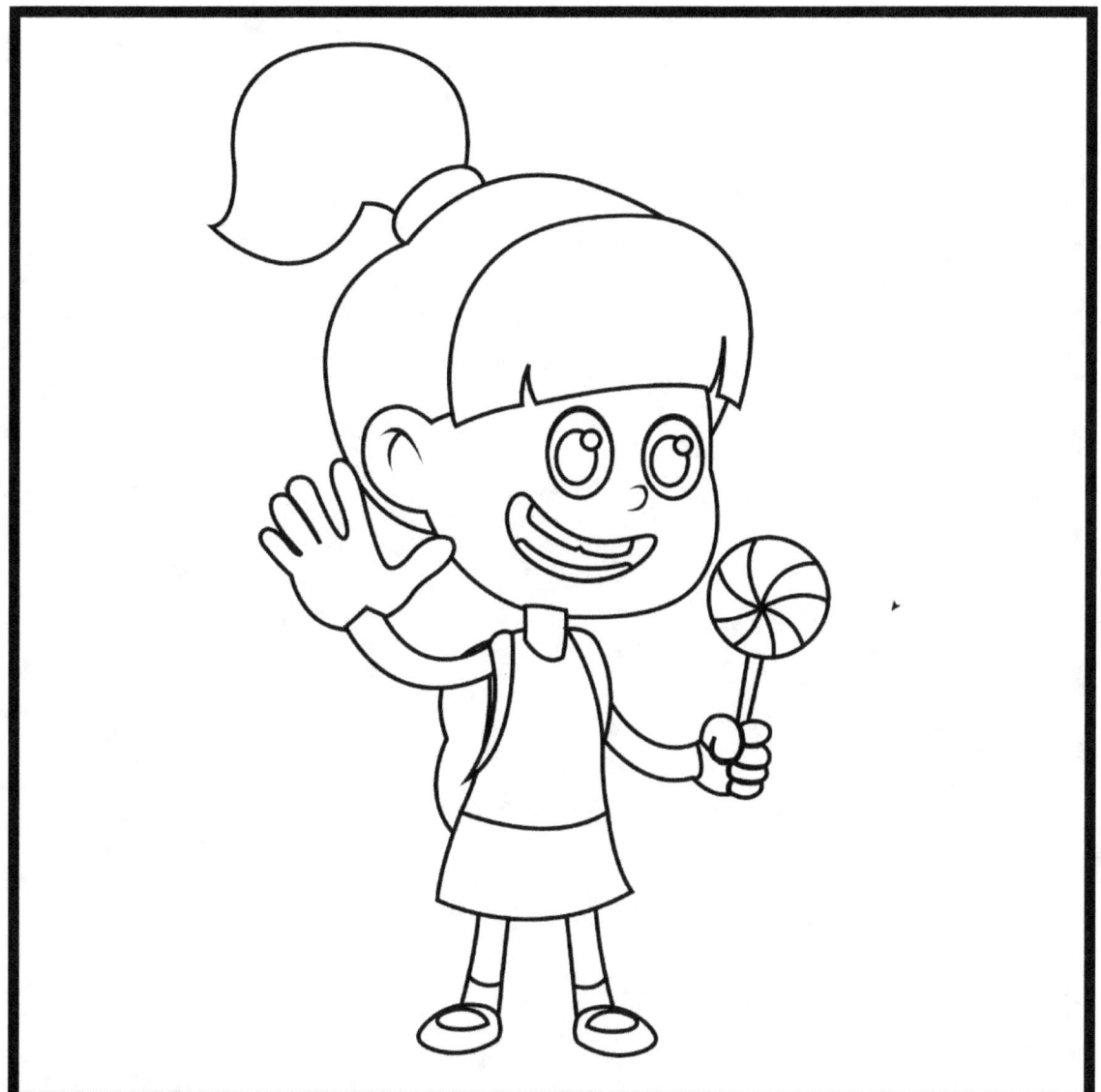

note:

_____

_____

_____

MARCH 39TH

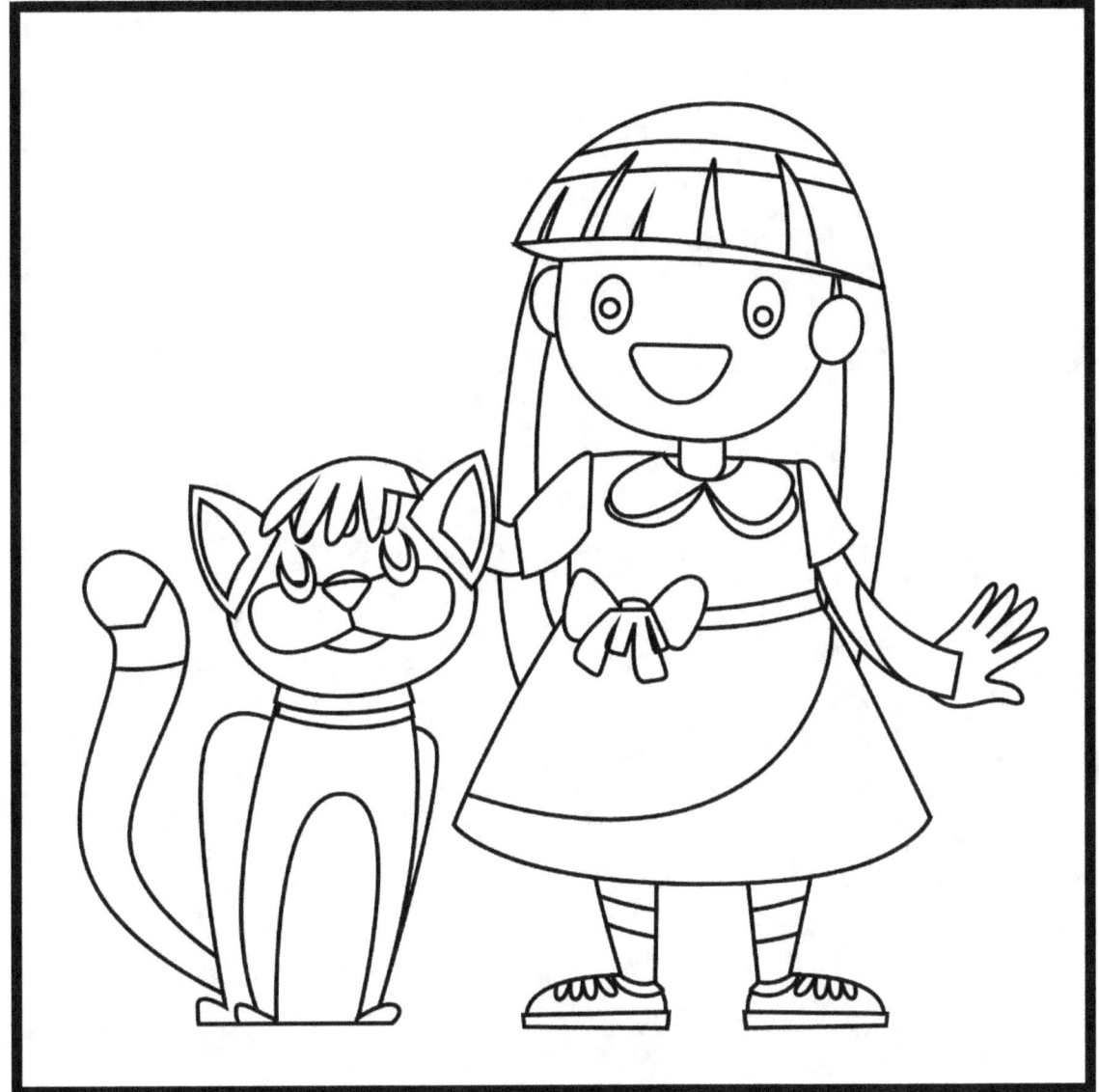

note:

_____

_____

_____

MARCH 40TH

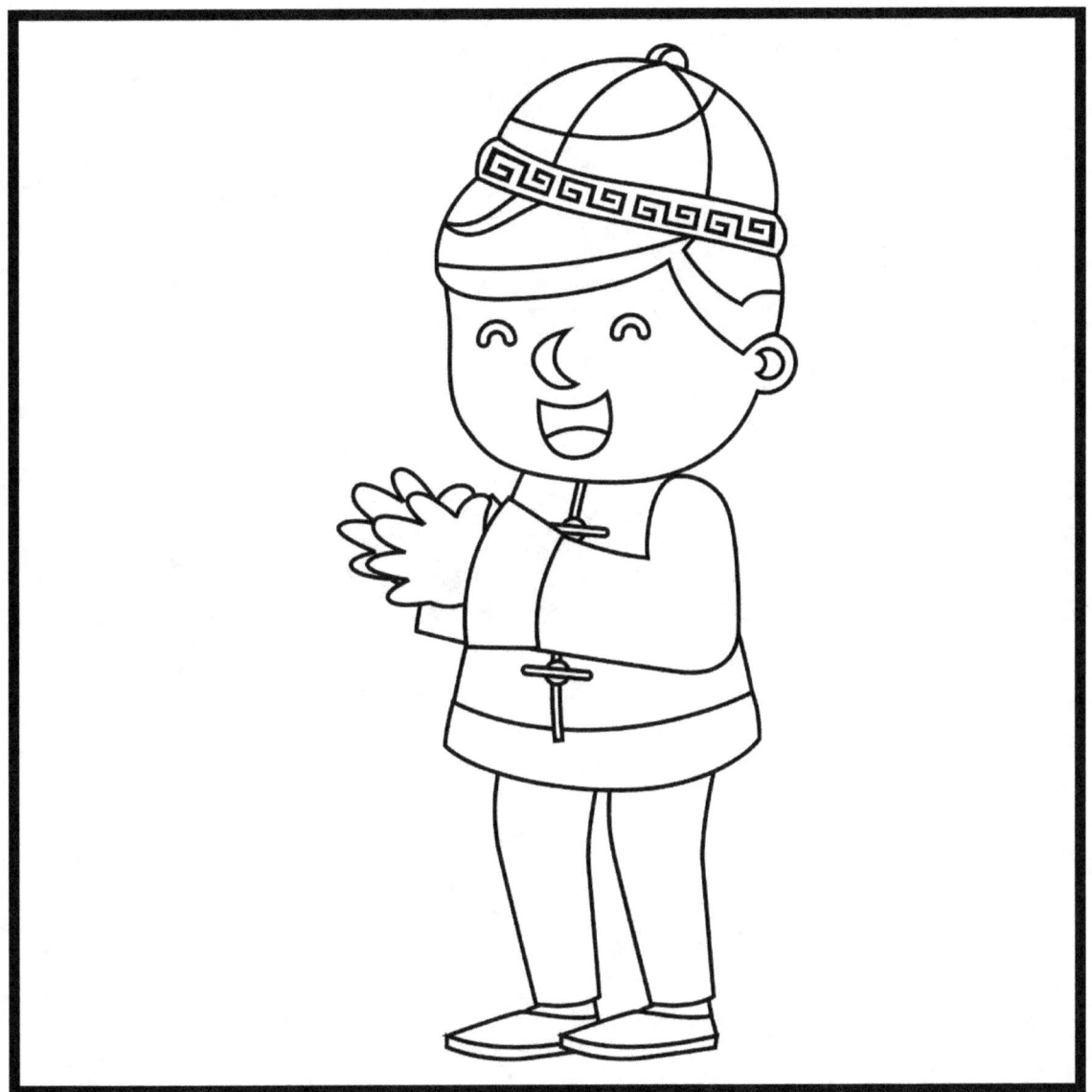

note:

_____

_____

_____

MARCH 41TH

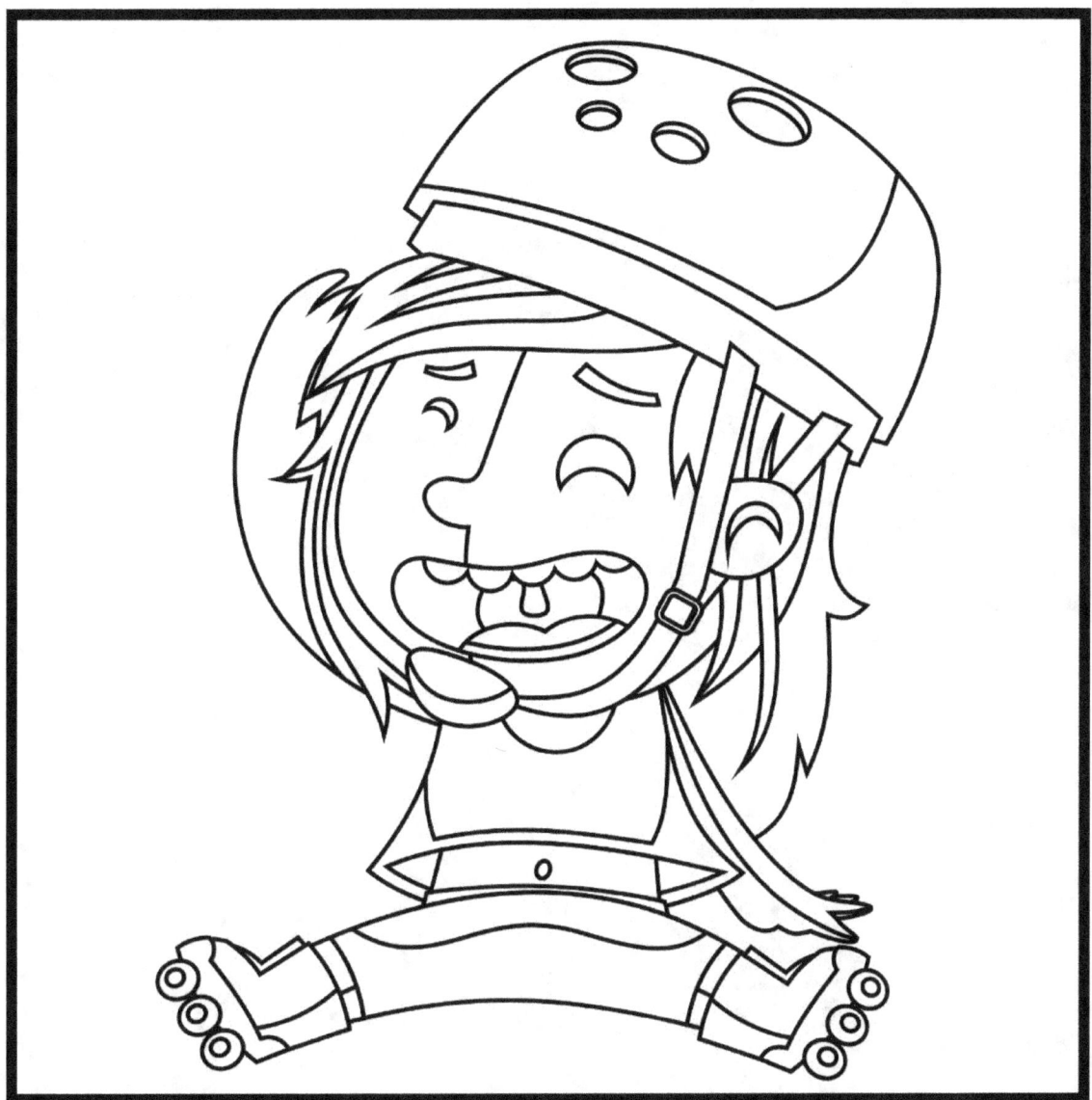

note:

_____

_____

_____

MARCH 42TH

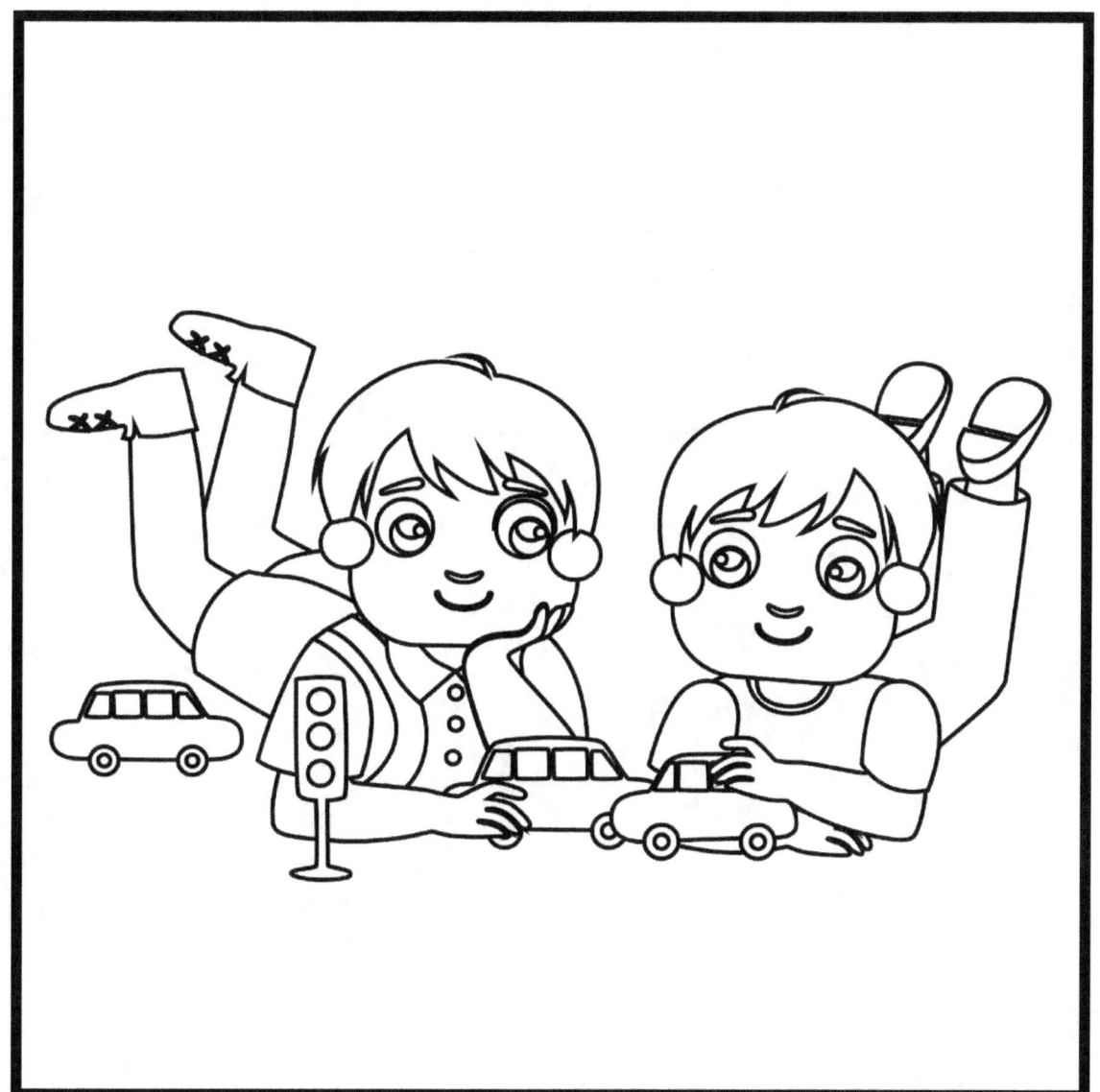

note:

_____

_____

_____

MARCH 43TH

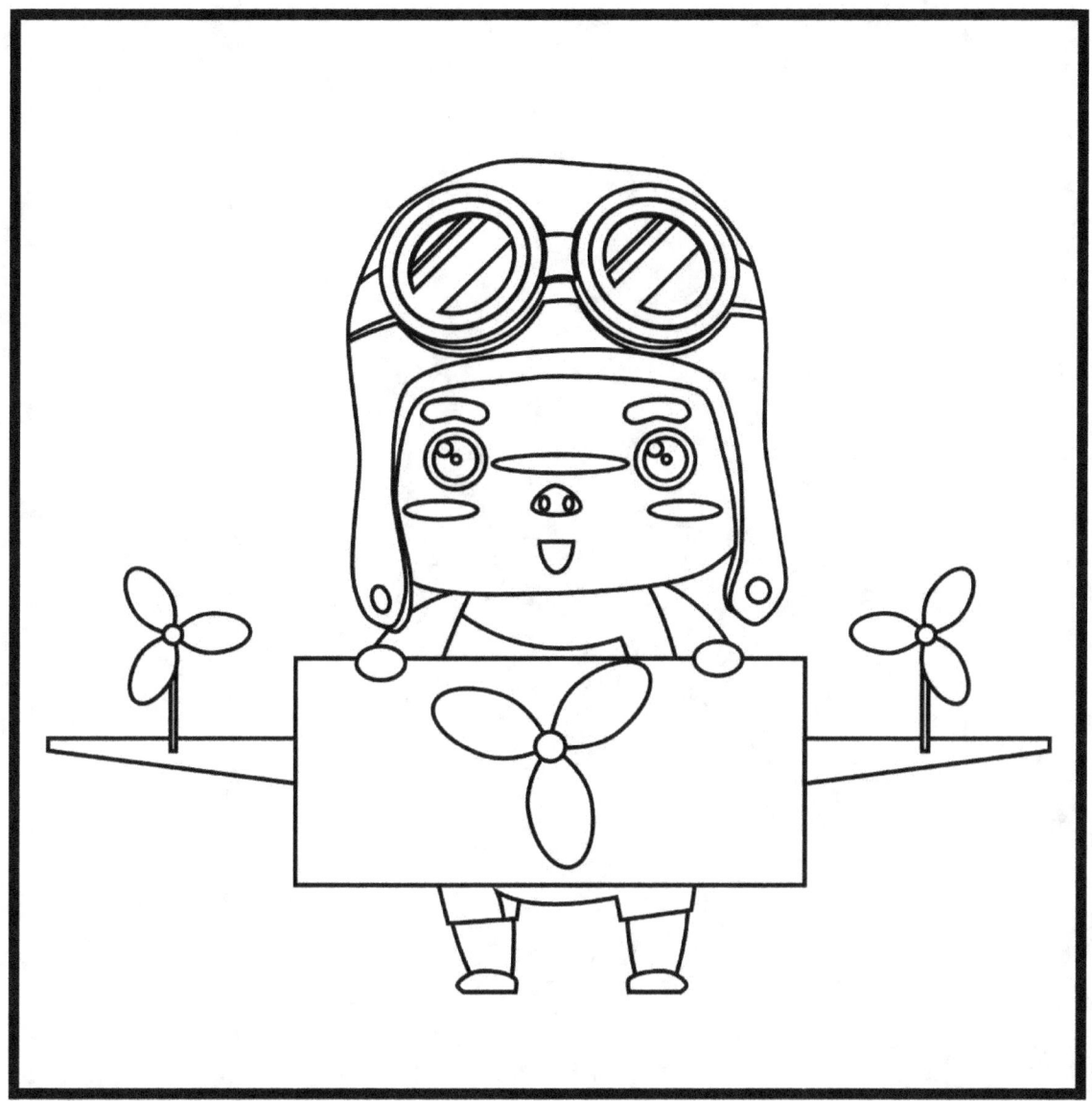

note:

_____

_____

_____

MARCH 44TH

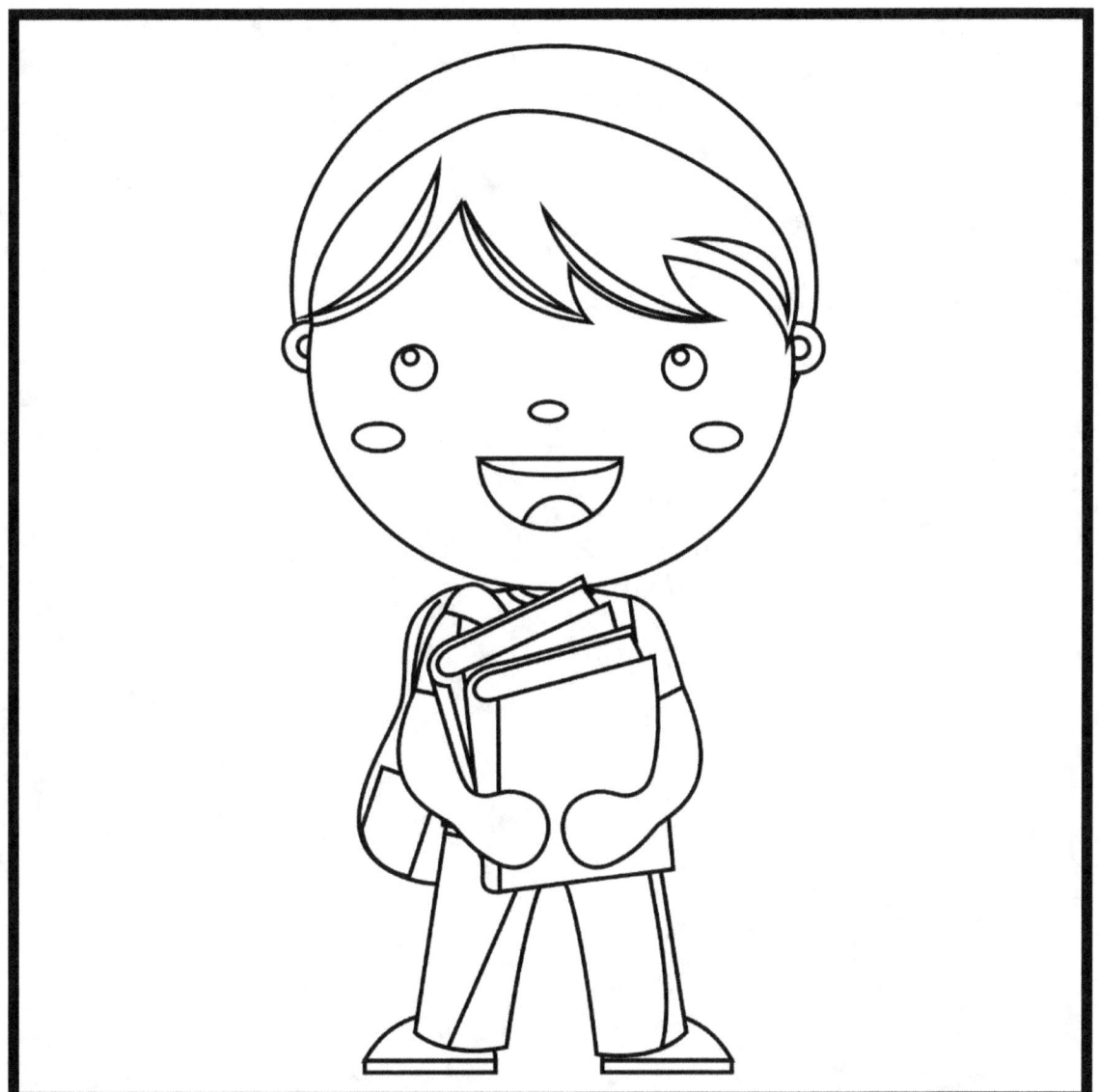

note:

_____

_____

_____

MARCH 45TH

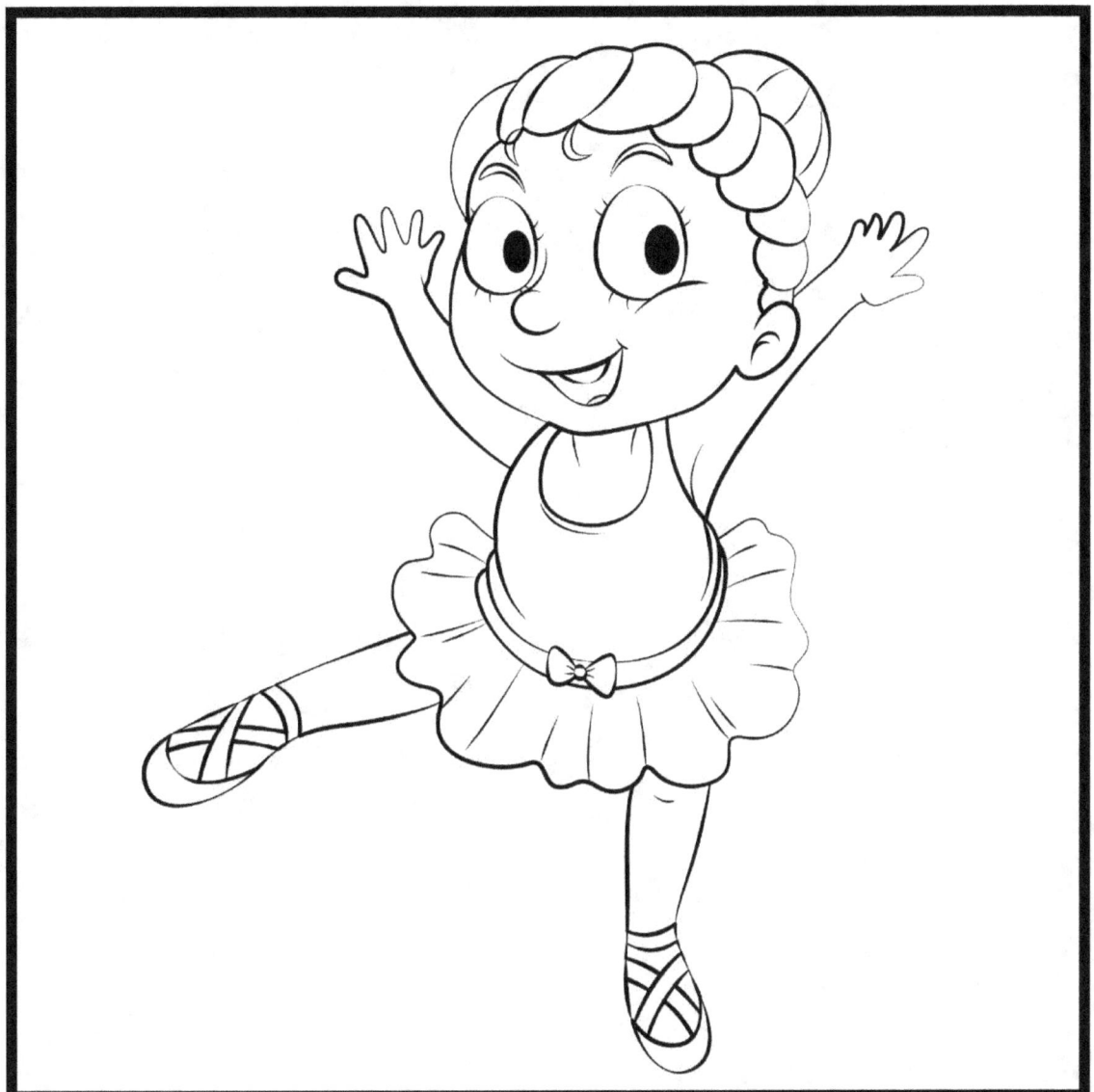

note:

_____

_____

_____

MARCH 46TH

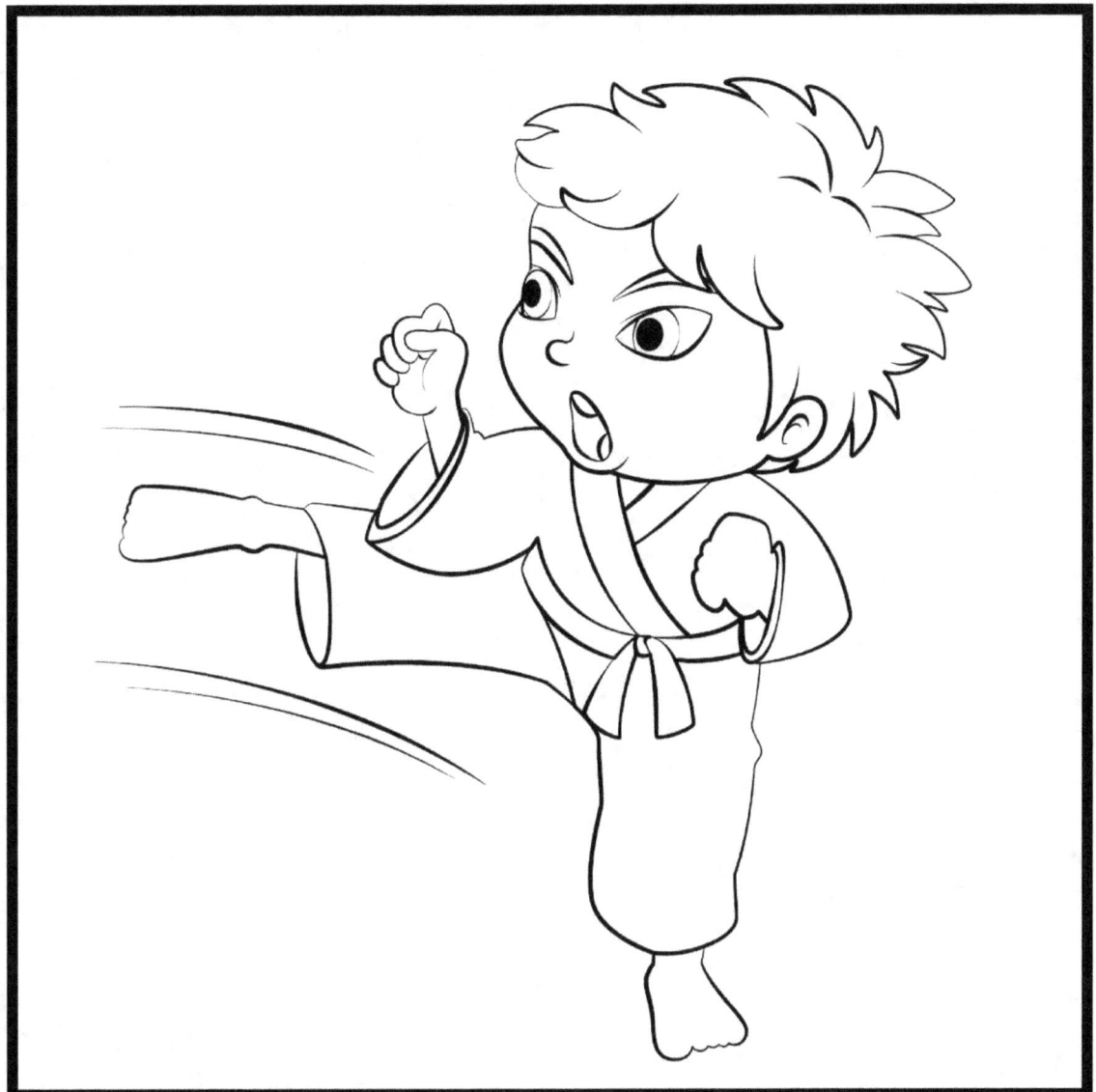

note:

_____

_____

_____

MARCH 47TH

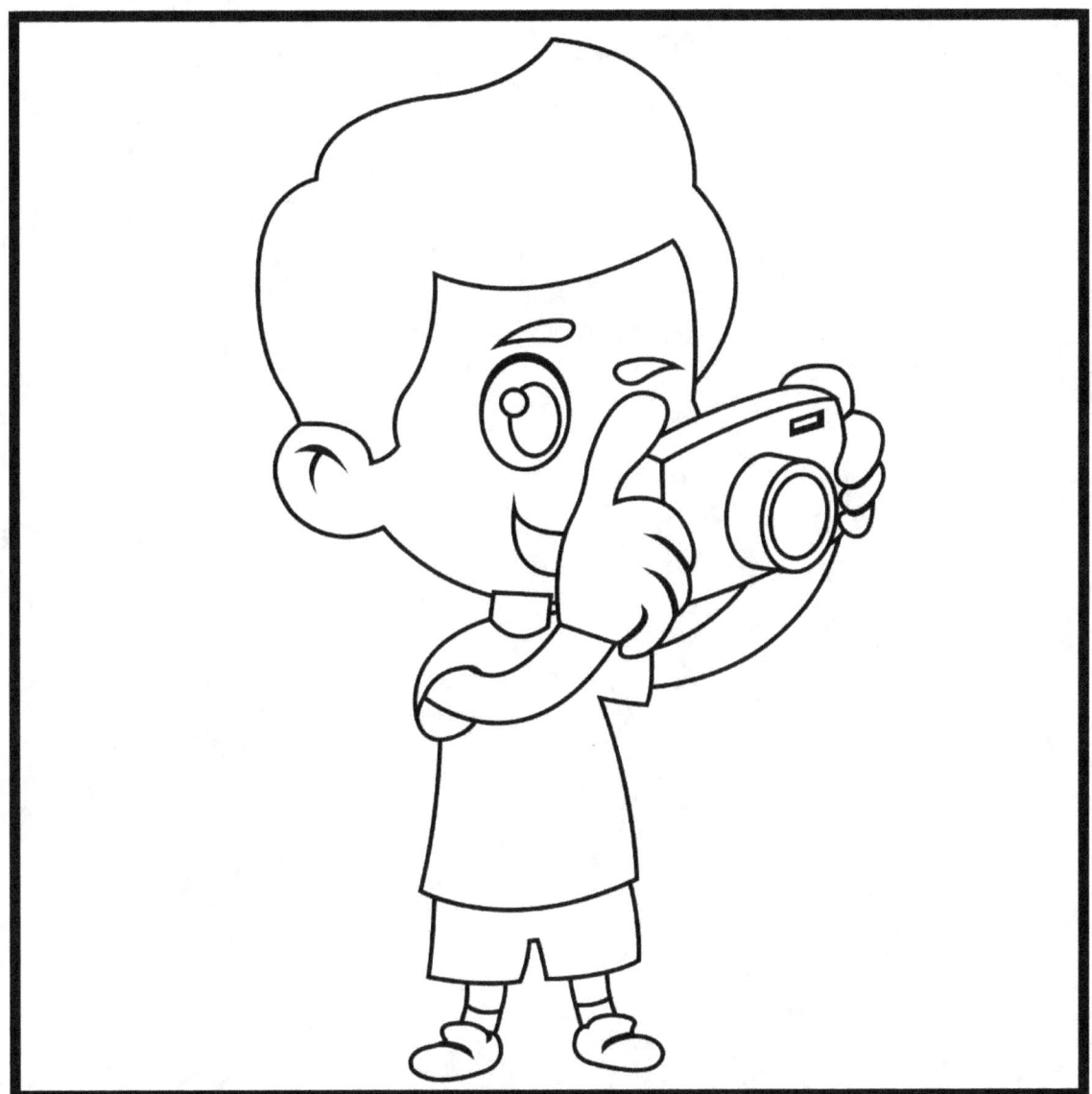

note:

_____

_____

_____

MARCH 48TH

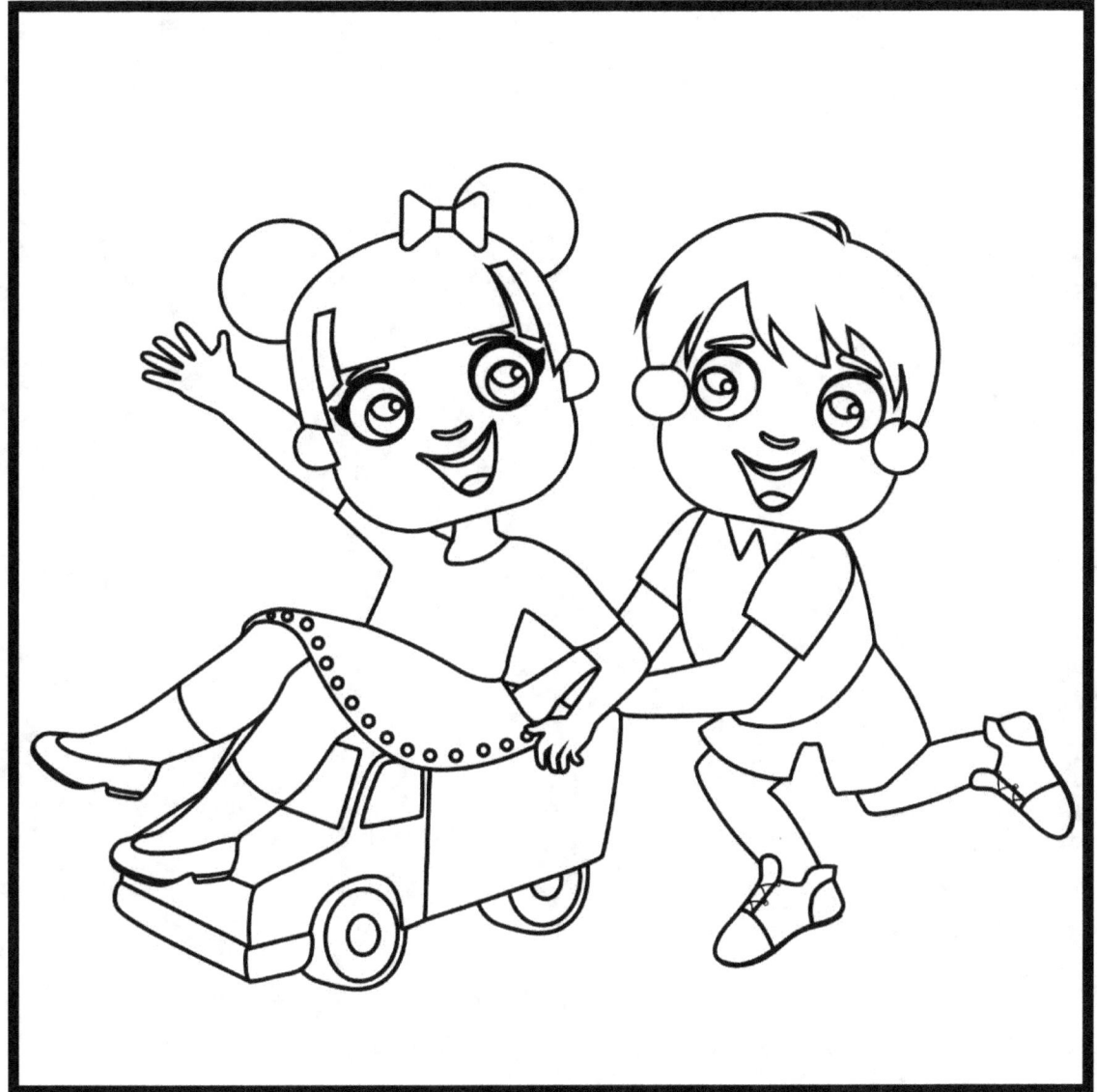

note:

_____

_____

_____

MARCH 49TH

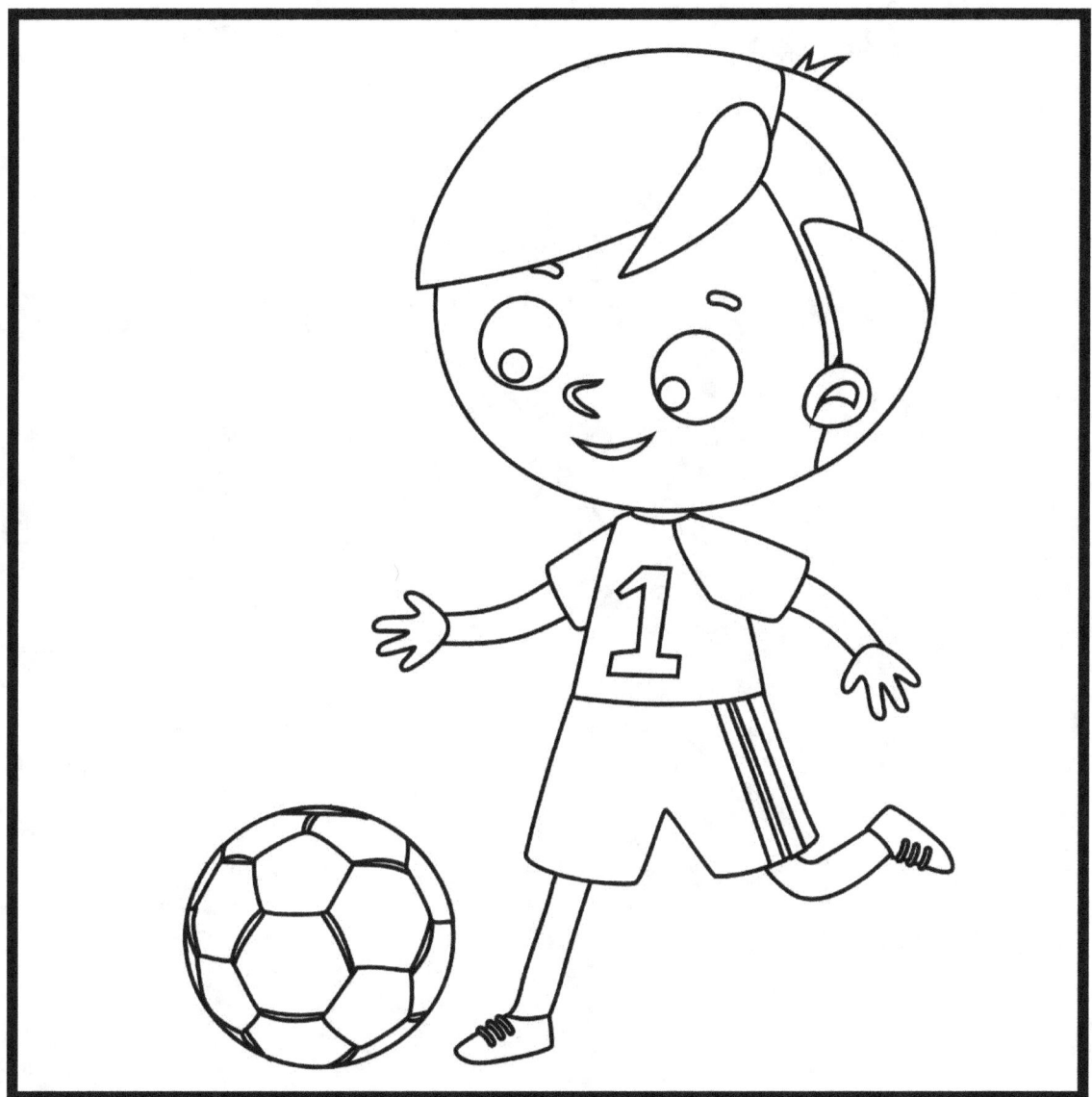

note:

_____

_____

_____

MARCH 50TH

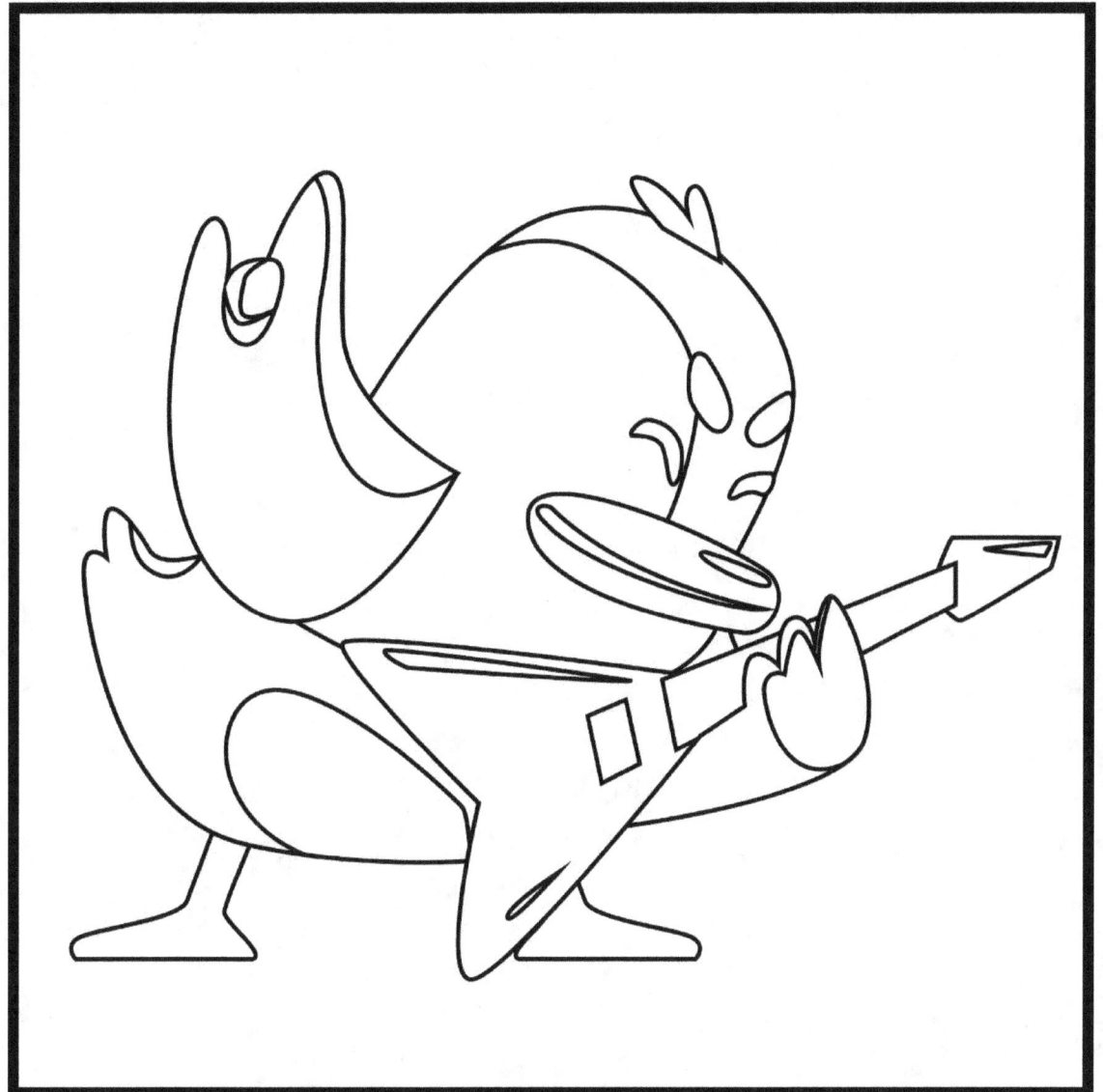

note:

_____

_____

_____